Alternatives for Long-Range Ground-Attack Systems

March 2006

The Congress of the United States ■ Congressional Budget Office

Note

The cover shows the three types of long-range bombers in service with the United States Air Force. From the top: the B-2A Spirit stealth bomber (USAF photo by Master Sgt. Val Gempis); the B-1B Lancer (USAF photo by Master Sgt. Robert W. Valenca); and the B-52H Stratofortress (USAF photo by Master Sgt. Michael A. Kaplan).

Preface

The recent air campaigns in Afghanistan and Iraq highlighted the utility of long-range ground-attack systems. The Air Force's fleet of B-52, B-1, and B-2 heavy bombers helped coalition forces overcome the limited availability of local air bases by operating from more distant bases and provided responsive air support to ground forces by orbiting over the battlefield for long periods of time. Recognizing those contributions, the Department of Defense (DoD) is in the process of developing new concepts for the role of long-range systems in future conflicts and is also beginning to examine new systems that could be used to attack targets anywhere in the world.

This Congressional Budget Office (CBO) study—prepared at the request of the Subcommittee on Strategic Forces of the Senate Committee on Armed Services—looks at the capabilities and costs associated with alternative long-range strike systems that DoD might develop and procure to improve its ability to conduct ground-attack operations. The study compares the advantages, disadvantages, and costs of eight alternative systems—five aircraft-based systems and three missile-based systems. In keeping with CBO's mandate to provide objective, impartial analysis, this study makes no recommendations.

Robie Samanta Roy and David Arthur of CBO's National Security Division prepared the study under the supervision of J. Michael Gilmore. (Robie Samanta Roy has since left CBO.) David Newman, Raymond Hall, and Matthew Schmit of CBO's Budget Analysis Division prepared the cost estimates and wrote the appendix under the supervision of Jo Ann Vines. Kevin Perese and Adebayo Adedeji of CBO and Dr. Mitch Nikolich of CACI-NSR, Inc., provided thoughtful comments. (The assistance of an external participant implies no responsibility for the final product, which rests solely with CBO.)

Janey Cohen edited the study, and John Skeen proofread it. Christian Spoor edited the figures, and Leah Mazade edited the tables. Cynthia Cleveland produced drafts of the study and formatted the tables. Maureen Costantino designed the cover and prepared the study for publication, and Lenny Skutnik printed the initial copies.

Donald B. Marron
Acting Director

March 2006

Contents

Tables

Figures

Figures (Continued)

Summary

The United States maintains a considerable capability to attack ground targets with conventional weapons anywhere in the world. Air Force, Navy, and Marine Corps tactical aircraft deployed to forward locations can be used for ground attack, or "strike" missions, in the region where their bases or aircraft carriers are located, and a similar regional capability is offered by Tomahawk cruise missiles launched from submarines or surface ships. If air bases or aircraft carriers are not available in the region, long-range strike capability can be provided by the Air Force's smaller fleet of long-range bombers, which can conduct missions from more-distant bases, including ones in the United States.

The performance of the bomber force in Afghanistan (Operation Enduring Freedom) and Iraq (Operation Iraqi Freedom) confirmed the value of long-range strike systems that are less dependent on having access to air bases close to the conflict. In Afghanistan, strike aircraft were forced to fly very long missions with extensive airborne tanker support—fighters typically had to refuel many times during a mission—because of basing and airspace restrictions in neighboring countries. In Operation Iraqi Freedom, the availability of air bases was limited, and the air bases in Kuwait were vulnerable to attack by Iraqi cruise and ballistic missiles. Although both air campaigns were successful, if air operations of greater intensity or length had been needed, those adverse circumstances might have posed problems. In contrast, long-range bombers contributed to the campaigns over great distances from secure bases by operating from places such as Diego Garcia, an island in the Indian Ocean.

Although the Air Force continues to upgrade the existing bomber fleet to deliver most types of conventional weapons and to participate more effectively in tactical ground-attack operations, until recently there have not been definitive plans for expanding long-range strike capabilities. Numerous studies of which capabilities might be desired and several plans for potential long-range systems had been proposed, but none had resulted in decisions on a way to move forward.[1] Now, however, the Department of Defense (DoD) has begun to define initial plans for developing new long-range strike systems. For example, the 2006 Quadrennial Defense Review (QDR) report states that DoD intends to develop a new land-based long-range strike capability and to deploy an initial capability to deliver precision-guided conventional warheads using long-range ballistic missiles. However, because specific requirements for system performance and force levels have yet to be defined, considerable uncertainty remains as to which capabilities DoD will require of new long-range strike systems, how well different types of systems might provide those capabilities, and what it might cost to develop and deploy such systems.

This Congressional Budget Office (CBO) study, which was prepared before the release of the 2006 QDR, examines those questions. It compares how well eight long-range strike systems might perform in several areas that DoD studies have identified as important for future operations. Those systems reflect general classes of long-range weapons that have been proposed within the defense community and include aircraft, long-range missiles, and space-based weapons. Although all of the systems CBO examined would have the common characteristic of a range no less than about 1,500 nautical miles (nm)—greater than that of current or planned strike fighters carrying typical weapon loads—their performance in other

---

1. See, for example, Office of the Secretary of Defense, *Report to Congress on: Prompt Global Strike Plan* (June 2005); and Department of Defense, *Defense Planning Guidance: Long Range Global Precision Engagement Study* (April 2003).

Summary Table 1.

Long-Range Strike Alternatives Examined by CBO

	Unrefueled Range with Full Payload[a] (Nautical miles)	Payload[b] (Pounds)	Speed (Mach)
1 Arsenal Aircraft			
C-17	1,500	134,000	0.76
Supersonic missile	500	n.a.	3
2 Medium-Range Subsonic Bomber	1,500	20,000	0.85
3 Medium-Range Supersonic Dash Bomber	1,500	10,000	0.85 (Sustained) 1.5 (Dash)
4 Long-Range Subsonic Bomber	2,500	40,000	0.85
5 Long-Range Supersonic Cruise Bomber	2,500	40,000	2.4
6 Medium-Range Surface-Based CAV	3,200	2,000	14
7 Long-Range Surface-Based CAV	Global	4,000	20
8 Space-Based CAV	Nearly Global [c]	2,000	20

Source: Congressional Budget Office.

Note: CAV = common aero vehicle; n.a. = not applicable.

a.   The ranges shown are the maximum distance from an air base or launcher location to the target. For the aircraft alternatives, the total distance flown on an unrefueled mission would be double the values shown.

b.   Aircraft payloads represent combat loads; CAV payloads are per missile.

c.   From an equatorial orbit, space-based CAVs could reach any point on Earth between the latitudes of 60 degrees north and 60 degrees south.

areas would differ substantially, as would the estimated costs to develop and procure them.[2]

To compare the military utility of different approaches for striking at long range, CBO used several specific measures to quantify the types of capabilities that have been identified for future long-range strike systems:

■   Reach—the ability to attack targets regardless of location.

■   Responsiveness—the ability to attack targets quickly.

■   Firepower—the ability to sustain attacks over time.

■   Survivability—the ability to avoid or defeat air defenses.

CBO did not assess how much of the particular capabilities might be desired or needed but rather compared how well its alternatives (as well as today's forces) could provide them.

Alternatives for Improving Long-Range Strike Capabilities

The eight alternatives examined by CBO represent very diverse approaches to improving long-range strike capabilities (see Summary Table 1). Each offers advantages and disadvantages in how it contributes to the ability to strike at long range.

2.   Unless it is specified otherwise, an aircraft's range in this study refers to its combat radius with a full load. The combat radius is defined here as the distance that an aircraft could fly from its base to attack a target and still have enough fuel to return without aerial refueling. The total distance the aircraft would fly on such a mission would be twice that range. Missile ranges are simply the maximum distance from the launch location to the target.

Alternative 1 would provide for the delivery of fast missiles from a large cargo aircraft, an approach that has been dubbed an "arsenal aircraft" in past studies. The system CBO examined would consist of a new supersonic missile capable of flying 500 nm at Mach 3 (three times the speed of sound) that would be launched by C-17 cargo aircraft with internal rack systems from which the missiles could be extracted through the aircraft's rear door. Aircraft from the planned fleet of 180 air mobility C-17s could carry the racks, or additional C-17s could be purchased and dedicated to the strike mission. Because cargo aircraft are not designed to elude air defenses, the arsenal aircraft itself could not penetrate hostile airspace. They would have to launch their missiles from secure airspace.

Alternative 2 and Alternative 3 would develop stealthy medium-range bombers capable of penetrating air defenses. Those aircraft would have ranges and payloads between those of today's strike fighters and long-range bombers. (The now-retired F-111 is a recent example of a U.S. medium-range bomber.) The aircraft in Alternative 2 would have a higher payload than that of Alternative 3 but would be limited to subsonic speeds. The aircraft in Alternative 3, a concept similar to proposals for a so-called FB-22, would be capable of dash speeds up to Mach 1.5 for limited distances. Those aircraft could be designed as either manned or unmanned systems. (CBO's cost estimates assume they would be manned.)

Alternative 4 and Alternative 5 would develop long-range bombers also capable of penetrating air defenses. Those aircraft would have ranges and payloads similar to those of today's heavy B-52, B-1, and B-2 bombers. Alternative 4's aircraft would be similar in concept (although not necessarily in specific design) to the stealthy, subsonic B-2. Alternative 5's aircraft would be an advanced bomber capable of maintaining speeds greater than Mach 2 over most of its mission. Achieving higher speed (with a similar range and payload) than that of Alternative 4 would require about a 40 percent larger and heavier aircraft to accommodate more fuel and more powerful engines. Although probably less stealthy than the other aircraft alternatives—its large size and other design characteristics for sustained supersonic flight are not as amenable to stealth—the high speed of the supersonic cruise bomber would contribute to its survivability. Those aircraft could also be designed as either manned or unmanned systems. (CBO's cost estimates assume they would be manned.)

Alternatives 6 through 8 would develop maneuvering warheads called common aero vehicles (CAVs) similar in concept to hypersonic systems that have been explored by the Defense Advanced Research Projects Agency and the Air Force under the FALCON (Force Application and Launch from the Continental United States) program. CAVs are missile- or spacecraft-launched unmanned vehicles capable of flying through space on suborbital trajectories. CAVs are shaped to generate sufficient lift so that, after reentering the atmosphere, they can glide many thousands of miles to their targets at hypersonic speeds with a combination of thrusters and flaps providing maneuvering control. CBO examined CAV systems that could be launched at their targets using a ground-based intercontinental ballistic missile (ICBM) or a smaller ground- or ship-based medium-range missile, as well as CAVs that would be placed in equatorial low-Earth orbits and de-orbited when needed.

The next section provides quantitative comparisons of the eight specific systems CBO analyzed. However, that analysis pointed to several general observations that can be made about each of the classes of systems CBO examined, independent of detailed design specifications:

Arsenal aircraft armed with supersonic missiles offer the potential to provide significant firepower and responsiveness at costs substantially lower than those of new penetrating bombers. However, their vulnerability to enemy air defenses would limit their reach into defended airspace to the range of the missile, a much shorter distance than those of the other alternatives CBO examined.

Stealthy manned or unmanned medium-range bombers would offer reach and firepower improvements over current long-range strike fighters but would not offer the global reach or long loitering capability of long-range bombers. (Loitering in the target area enables aircraft to respond very quickly to fleeting targets.) A greater number of medium-range bombers could be fielded for a given investment, although the net firepower would not necessarily be higher than that of a smaller number of larger-payload long-range bombers.[3]

Stealthy manned or unmanned long-range bombers offer global reach and substantial sustained firepower. Subsonic bombers would offer global response times on the order

---

3. See Chapter 4 for a comparison of the effects of purchasing different quantities of the penetrating bombers.

of 15 hours with long loitering endurance to provide fire against fleeting targets with response times on the order of several minutes. Supersonic bombers would offer shorter global response times but would have higher cost and might have a limited ability to loiter.

*Hypersonic CAVs—either space-based or launched by ballistic missiles—*would offer responsiveness on the order of one hour against targets anywhere on the globe and would be the most difficult systems for enemy defenses to intercept. However, their high unit cost implies that they probably could not be purchased in sufficient numbers to provide the sustained firepower offered by aircraft forces.

Comparison of Long-Range Strike Alternatives Considered by CBO

The long-range strike systems examined by CBO would provide diverse capabilities, with each alternative offering advantages and disadvantages for different types of missions. In addition to differences in capability, the alternatives would have unique implications for the future force structure. Fielding CAVs, for example, would provide a new rapid-strike capability but would not address the issue of the aging bomber force. Conversely, a supersonic bomber could replace today's bombers but would offer less responsiveness than CAVs would. Because of such distinctions, the alternatives CBO examined should not necessarily be viewed as independent alternatives. Depending on the specific requirements that DoD eventually establishes for its long-range strike systems, the preferred solution might include more than one of the systems CBO examined.

Capabilities

In comparing the capabilities of the alternative long-range strike systems, CBO examined how far each system could reach, how responsive it would be in several settings, how much firepower it could provide, and how safely it could operate in the face of enemy air defenses.

Reach. The reach of a long-range strike system can be important for two reasons. First, long range allows missions to be conducted from greater distances, either before local bases can be established or when they are not available. Aerial refueling, however, means that even short-range aircraft can fly missions much longer than their "unrefueled range" would allow. Consequently, all of CBO's alternatives would offer the potential for global reach.

Nonetheless, the two long-range CAVs and the two long-range bombers would be best suited for missions requiring global reach. The medium-range bomber alternatives could, in principle, be used for intercontinental missions, but the need for more frequent refueling would complicate operations, and crew endurance in the probably cramped confines of a small cockpit might present problems. The C-17 arsenal aircraft could carry relief crews to help remedy that problem, but it would still require more frequent refueling than would the long-range bomber alternatives. Although lacking inherent global reach, the medium-range CAV alternative could cover most of the globe from just a few forward land bases (for example, Guam in the western Pacific Ocean and Diego Garcia, a territory of Great Britain in the Indian Ocean) or ships.

A second facet to the military value of long range is the capability it offers to reach targets deep in hostile airspace, where support from airborne tankers would not be available. That can be important against larger countries or in situations where tanker operations are otherwise constrained. All of the alternatives CBO examined except the arsenal aircraft provide very good capability to reach any point within all or most countries in the world. The long-range bombers and the long-range surface-based CAV could do so for all countries. The medium-range bombers could do so for 95 percent of all countries under conservative assumptions about access to airspace adjacent to the target country. Easing those assumptions slightly would enable full coverage. The medium-range CAV could fully cover all countries given suitable launch locations. The space-based CAV could fully cover almost all countries (about 97 percent of them) from its equatorial orbit. The exceptions are those countries with territory at North or South latitudes greater than about 60 degrees. The arsenal aircraft, carrying a supersonic missile with a range of 500 nm after launch, would provide the least coverage. If the C-17 delivering the missile must stand off outside hostile airspace, it could fully cover only about 75 percent of the world's countries.[4]

---

4. This geography-based analysis does not distinguish among nations that are more or less likely to be considered potential threats. Such judgments are subjective and change over time. For three nations commonly mentioned as potential adversaries—North Korea, Iran, and China—the CAV and long-range bomber alternatives would provide total coverage, the medium-range bombers could not reach parts of China, and the supersonic air-launched missile could not reach parts of Iran and China.

Summary Figure 1.

Response Times of Alternative Strike Systems for Preplanned Missions

(Hours to strike target)

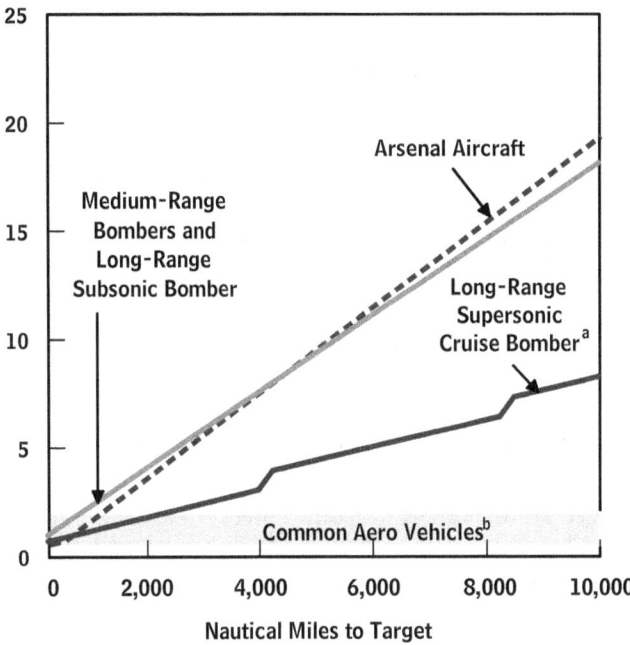

Source: Congressional Budget Office.

a.   The steps in the line for the supersonic cruise bomber result from its need to slow for aerial refueling.

b.   Response times for the common aero vehicle alternatives will vary for a given distance to the target, depending on the specific flight profile needed. The medium-range common aero vehicle has a maximum distance to target of 3,200 nautical miles.

Responsiveness. CBO considered responsiveness in two contexts: preplanned missions that would require responsiveness on the order of hours, and fleeting-target or ground-support missions that would require response times on the order of a few minutes. Assuming a similar planning process, a system's speed will be the primary determinant of its responsiveness in a preplanned mission. The greater the distance to be traveled, the greater the cumulative advantage of higher speed (see Summary Figure 1). The hypersonic CAV alternatives, consequently, would offer by far the shortest response times among CBO's alternatives. The long-range supersonic cruise bomber (Alternative 5) would have a response time between that of the CAVs and the other aircraft alternatives. The medium-range supersonic bomber would not be significantly more responsive than the subsonic aircraft

because it could not maintain supersonic speed during the entire transit to its target.

Against fleeting targets or in a ground-support role, none of the long-range strike alternatives would provide, from a standing start, response times on the order of a few minutes. Even a space-based CAV would need at least 15 minutes if the launcher was in the right orbital location and no atmospheric maneuvering was necessary. Very short response times require maintaining systems close to the locations where targets are expected to appear, a tactic that could not be accomplished with the CAV alternatives. For the other alternatives, the area that can be covered by an aircraft orbiting over a particular location for a given response time and the number of aircraft needed to maintain such orbits become the critical factors. (See Chapter 3 for a more detailed discussion.) From that perspective, the arsenal aircraft would provide the shortest response times with the fewest aircraft because the Mach 3 missile it would employ can dash much farther in a

Summary Figure 2.

Number of Aircraft Needed for 24-Hour Coverage of 25 Percent of Afghanistan with a 10-Minute Response Time

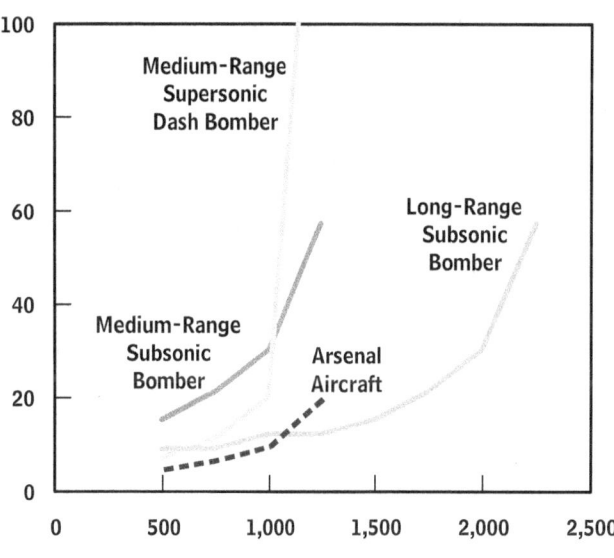

Source: Congressional Budget Office.

Note: This figure assumes that an aircraft expends all of its munitions before returning to base. Endurance would be lower if an aircraft returned with unused munitions.

Summary Figure 3.

Bomb Delivery Rates for Alternative Strike Aircraft

(Number of 2,000-pound JDAM-equivalents per aircraft per day)

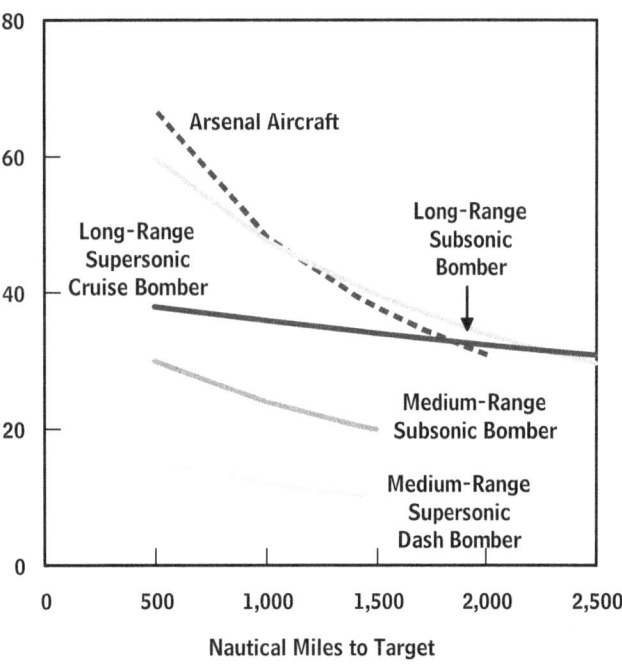

Source: Congressional Budget Office.

Note: Data are shown out to the unrefueled radius of each type of aircraft when carrying a full bomb load. All alternatives could achieve greater ranges with aerial refueling or reduced bomb loads.

JDAM = Joint Direct Attack Munition.

given amount of time than can the other aircraft alternatives (see Summary Figure 2). The long-range subsonic bomber (Alternative 4) would offer good performance because of its long endurance, especially for orbits far from base or far from aerial refueling support. Performance of the medium-range bomber alternatives suffers from the lack of the supersonic missile's high speed (Alternative 1) and the long-range subsonic bomber's endurance (Alternative 4), although the supersonic dash capability of Alternative 3 gives it good performance for orbits close to base. The supersonic cruise bomber could not meet the responsiveness criteria in Summary Figure 2 because CBO assumed its design would not be suitable for maintaining sustained low-speed orbits.

Firepower. Another requirement for long-range strike systems will probably be support of operations requiring the delivery of a high volume of munitions such as those seen in large conflicts. Long-range systems could be especially important early in those situations, before significant numbers of tactical aircraft have been deployed to the theater. Because of their large payloads, the arsenal aircraft and the long-range subsonic bomber (Alternatives 1 and 4) would offer the highest per-platform weapon delivery rates for mission distances of less than 2,400 nm (see Summary Figure 3). For mission distances of longer than 2,400 nm, the supersonic cruise bomber's speed would provide it an advantage in firepower despite the longer time needed to prepare it for each mission.[5]

The number of systems purchased also affects the achievable firepower. Although Alternative 1 can physically achieve a high weapon delivery rate, the relatively high cost of each supersonic missile—about $1.4 million per round as compared with about $31,000 for a satellite-guided bomb such as the Joint Direct Attack Munition (JDAM)—may ultimately constrain its use. CBO did not include the CAV alternatives in the firepower comparison because their much higher unit costs would almost certainly make them unsuitable for such sustained operations. Similarly, the number of aircraft purchased under a given alternative would affect the forcewide weapon delivery capability. For example, an additional 25 medium-range subsonic bombers (for a total of 300) would provide similar firepower (albeit over shorter distances) as the 150 long-range bombers under Alternative 4 but for about $19 billion less. In contrast, 600 medium-range supersonic bombers would be needed to provide an equivalent firepower at a cost of about $38 billion more than that for 150 long-range subsonic bombers.

Survivability. The ability to reach the target—and, in the case of aircraft, return safely—in the face of air defenses is important for long-range strike systems because they will most likely be tasked in circumstances where the timely suppression of enemy air defenses will not be possible. The CAV alternatives examined by CBO would have the greatest survivability. After launch, their hypersonic speeds and ability to maneuver unpredictably could only be countered by a very sophisticated missile defense sys-

---

5.   CBO assumed that the greater complexity of a supersonic cruising aircraft and the greater rigors of sustained supersonic flight would result in servicing times between missions of about twice the length of the long-range subsonic-bomber alternative.

Summary Table 2.

Estimated Costs of Long-Range Strike Alternatives Examined by CBO

| | Quantity | Costs[a] (Billions of 2006 dollars) | | | Average Unit Procurement Cost (Millions of 2006 dollars) |
		RDT&E	Procurement	Total[b]	
1 Arsenal Aircraft	2,000 [c]	1.5	2.8/6.1 [c]	4.3/7.6 [c]	1.4 [d]
2 Medium-Range Subsonic Bomber	275	19	52	72	188
3 Medium-Range Supersonic Dash Bomber	275	23	61	85	220
4 Long-Range Subsonic Bomber	150	31	61	93	409
5 Long-Range Supersonic Cruise Bomber	150	69	137	207	912
6 Medium-Range Surface-Based CAV	48	2.4	1.2	3.7	26
7 Long-Range Surface-Based CAV [e]	24	2.5	0.9	4.0	36
8 Space-Based CAV	128 [f]	4.0	7.7	11.7	55

Source: Congressional Budget Office.

Note: RDT&E = research, development, test, and evaluation; CAV = common aero vehicle.

a.   The costs for Alternatives 2 to 5 exclude munitions.

b.   Includes additional military construction costs of about $1 billion for the aircraft alternatives (2 to 5) and $600 million for Alternative 7.

c.   The quantity shown is the number of supersonic missiles purchased. The lower of the two costs assumes that those missiles would be carried by C-17 aircraft in the current fleet. The higher of the two costs assumes that 15 additional C-17s would be purchased to support the strike mission.

d.   Average unit procurement cost is for supersonic missiles only.

e.   Alternative 7 assumes that 24 Peacekeeper missiles would be converted to carry two CAVs per missile. If more missiles were desired, as many as 60 Peacekeepers might be available for conversion. The cost of additional missiles would be much higher than the cost shown here because new boosters would be needed.

f.   Enough satellites would be purchased to maintain the constellation for 30 years. Only 40 space-based CAVs would be available for use at any one time.

tem. Attacking CAVs before they were launched would be difficult as well: survivable long-range systems would be needed to hit the surface-based CAV systems, and an antisatellite capability would be needed against orbiting CAVs. In the case of the arsenal aircraft, although the supersonic air-launched missile would also be a challenge for air defenses, its C-17 delivery platform could be vulnerable if an adversary was able to send fighters out to intercept it. The stealth designs for the subsonic bombers, Alternative 2 and Alternative 4, should give them good survivability against ground-based air defenses and against fighters at night. They could be vulnerable to fighters during the day, however, when the bombers

could be detected visually. The long-range supersonic cruise bomber has a combination of limited stealth and high speed that should enable it to avoid engagement by many surface defenses and to outrun fighters sent to intercept it. Similarly, the medium-range bomber in Alternative 3 could use stealth to survive surface defenses and its supersonic dash speed to elude fighters, although with less certainty because it would have less of a speed advantage than the supersonic cruise bomber would.

Cost and Force-Structure Implications

Comparing the long-range strike alternatives is complicated by the significant differences in the estimated costs to develop and field them (see Summary Table 2). CBO estimates that research, development, test, and evaluation (RDT&E) costs could vary by more than an order of magnitude among the alternatives, with the arsenal aircraft and CAV alternatives costing the least and the advanced supersonic cruise bomber the most. Similarly, estimates of production costs also vary over a broad range, although the differences among alternatives are in part the result of assumptions about how many of each type of system would be purchased. The cost estimates are presented in 2006 dollars. Significant uncertainty exists about the costs associated with developing, purchasing, and operating weapon systems envisioned in the alternatives because those programs are either conceptual in nature or in the early stages of development. Consequently, they entail a greater risk of cost and schedule overruns than do programs that are better defined and based on proven technologies. CBO's cost estimates represent one possible outcome, calculated under specific assumptions.

Without established DoD requirements as a guide, CBO based its estimates of procurement quantities for each alternative on the current force structure and force-structure plans wherever possible. Procurement quantities were not adjusted to try to achieve equivalent capabilities. (For example, the 40 operational CAVs purchased under each CAV alternative would be equivalent to the payloads of only about two long-range bombers.) Details of CBO's methods for developing its cost estimates are described in the appendix.

In general, the alternatives that involve penetrating bombers—Alternatives 2, 3, 4, and 5—are much more expensive to develop and procure, but they offer the advantage of being able to repeatedly deliver relatively inexpensive munitions. The very short response times of the CAV alternatives come with the disadvantage of high unit costs, which could limit the number procured.

Arsenal Aircraft. The arsenal-aircraft alternative would be less costly than the penetrating-bomber alternatives and less costly than the CAVs on a per-missile basis, although as noted earlier, the arsenal aircraft would have several drawbacks. It would, however, represent a new type of strike system not comparable with any of today's systems. The lower cost shown in Summary Table 2 assumes that aircraft could be drawn from the Air Force's planned inventory of 180 C-17s purchased for strategic airlift. If purchases of more C-17s dedicated only to strike missions were necessary, the cost of this alternative would be

higher. For example, 15 new aircraft would cost an additional $3.3 billion, CBO estimates. Such additional aircraft would be able to augment the airlift fleet when not needed as strike aircraft.

Medium-Range Bombers. The costs for the medium-range bombers in Alternatives 2 and 3 are based on purchasing 275 of those aircraft, a number similar to the current inventory of F-117 and F-15E strike fighters that a medium-range bomber might augment or replace.[6] Replacing those strike fighters with medium-range bombers would represent an improvement in strike capability because the new aircraft would have longer range, and all of them would be stealthy. (Only the 55 F-117s are stealthy today.) Although the current F-117s and F-15Es are aging, that force is not as old as today's long-range bombers. Because the aircraft in Alternatives 2 and 3 would have limited ability to conduct global-range strikes, they would leave unaddressed the issue of replacing today's long-range bombers. Thus, DoD might have to consider developing a new long-range bomber at some other time, or it could consider ceding the global-range mission to the lower-cost CAV alternatives.

Long-Range Bombers. The costs for the long-range bombers associated with Alternatives 4 and 5 are based on purchasing 150 of those aircraft, a number similar to the current long-range bomber force, and they could be used to either augment or replace those aircraft. Those new bombers, when coupled with the improved range expected for the Joint Strike Fighter over the F-16s that aircraft is expected to replace, could reduce the need for a direct replacement for the F-117 and F-15E forces. Alternatives 4 and 5 would maintain a manned global-strike capability, although CAVs might still be desired because of their much shorter response times.

Hypersonic CAVs. The alternatives associated with hypersonic CAVs that were examined by CBO would have significantly lower costs than those for the penetrating-bomber alternatives. CAVs have the disadvantages, however, of being less flexible than aircraft and very costly to purchase in more than limited numbers. CBO estimates, for example, that it would cost over $200 billion to purchase enough space-based CAVs to provide the same number of weapons as one day's delivery of 2,000-pound

---

6. The F-117 and F-15E are the longer-range tactical strike aircraft in the Air Force. The bulk of the force is made up of shorter-range F-16 multirole fighters.

JDAMs by 100 supersonic cruise bombers flying missions against targets 7,000 nm from their base. CBO sized its CAV alternatives on the basis of the availability of Peacekeeper ICBM boosters to launch them. Of course, larger numbers could be purchased, although at a higher unit cost because new boosters would have to be designed and built. Because the procurement quantities of space-based CAVs or ballistic missiles armed with CAVs would probably be limited by their high unit costs, those missiles would be unable to fully replace aircraft in the role of sustained long-range strike operations.

The United States' Long-Range Strike Capabilities

The U.S. military possesses considerable capability to attack targets anywhere in the world with conventional weapons. Shorter-range Air Force and Navy tactical aircraft, forward deployed and supported by airborne tankers, can attack targets in the region where their bases or aircraft carriers are located, and Tomahawk cruise missiles launched from submarines or surface ships offer a similar regional capability. If nearby air bases or aircraft carriers are not available, global reach can be achieved with the Air Force's smaller fleet of long-range bombers supported by airborne tankers.[1] Tactical ground-attack aircraft were used very effectively in Operation Desert Storm in 1991, where approximately 900 U.S. strike fighters based in the Persian Gulf region or on aircraft carriers nearby flew more than 40,000 ground-attack sorties against targets in Iraq during the 43-day air campaign. Bomber contributions, although important, were limited because only B-52 aircraft were available to deliver conventional munitions at that time. (Of the other two bomber types in today's inventory, the B-1 was not used, and the B-2 was not yet operational.)

Despite the effectiveness of the Desert Storm air campaign, planners saw a potential vulnerability in its execution. The heavy reliance on shorter-range tactical aircraft suggested that U.S. airpower could be severely limited if local air bases were unavailable. That scenario could occur if nations in a region were reluctant to host U.S. military forces, if operations had to take place in an undeveloped area that lacked such bases (or proximity to the sea for aircraft carriers), or if an adversary was able to attack bases hosting U.S. aircraft with ballistic or cruise missiles. Some planners argued that enlarging long-range strike forces would mitigate that vulnerability because such systems could be based farther away without an overreliance on aerial refueling. Having a greater number of long-range strike aircraft also would increase the number of airfields where strike aircraft could be based, and those bases could be beyond the range of an adversary's missiles.

A decade later, the experiences in Operation Enduring Freedom (Afghanistan) and Iraqi Freedom confirmed the value of long-range strike systems that are less dependent on having access to air bases close to the conflict. In the case of Afghanistan, basing and airspace restrictions forced strike aircraft to fly very long missions with extensive airborne tanker support. (Fighters typically had to refuel several times during a mission.) Against Iraq, strike fighters operating from air bases in Kuwait were within range of Iraqi cruise and ballistic missiles. Although both air campaigns were ultimately successful, those adverse circumstances might have posed serious problems, especially if air operations of greater size or length had been needed. In contrast, long-range bombers operating from Diego Garcia, an island in the Indian Ocean, contributed to those campaigns at long ranges from a secure base and with less reliance on airborne tanker support.[2] Navy aircraft operating from aircraft carriers also contributed to a greater relative extent than they did in Desert Storm.

Although the Department of Defense (DoD) is pursuing numerous programs to improve its strike capabilities, most are focused on modernizing the shorter-range strike fighter force or developing more capable munitions. Notable among those efforts are the F/A-18E/F and Joint Strike Fighter aircraft, which are scheduled to replace most Air Force, Navy, and Marine Corps strike fighters over the next 20 years or so. Although those fighter pro-

---

1. Intercontinental ballistic missiles also offer global reach but currently only for nuclear warheads.

2. Bombers were usually refueled in flight as well but not as frequently.

grams have been in existence for more than a decade, attention is now being given to improving long-range strike capabilities. Beginning in the 1990s, the existing bomber fleet was progressively upgraded so that it could deliver most types of conventional weapons, and the bombers were also equipped with the communications gear necessary to take part in tactical ground-attack operations. Those types of upgrades continue today. Until recently, however, there were no firm plans to expand the bomber force or to develop alternative means for conducting conventional strike missions over extended ranges. The Air Force has recently begun to examine a variety of strike alternatives with longer range than tactical fighters have, including a new medium-range bomber and intercontinental ballistic missiles (ICBMs) armed with conventional warheads. Additionally, the 2006 Quadrennial Defense Review (QDR) report states that DoD intends to develop a new long-range strike capability based on land and to deploy an initial capability to deliver conventional warheads with ballistic missiles fired from Trident submarines.

This Congressional Budget Office (CBO) study looks at the potential operational effectiveness and costs of alternatives for improving strike capabilities at combat ranges longer than about 1,500 nautical miles (nm) without refueling—ranges that are greater than those of current or planned strike fighters carrying typical weapon loads.[3] The study considers a spectrum of systems including aircraft, air- and surface-launched missiles, and space-based weapons. It compares the capabilities offered by such systems with one another as well as to existing means of providing the same military capability. The alternatives CBO examined reflect general classes of weapon systems, not specific systems proposed by DoD or by industry. They are not intended to identify a preferred solution but rather to offer a comparison of the capabilities and costs that can be expected from different types of long-range strike systems.

---

3. Unless it is specified otherwise, an aircraft's range in this study refers to its combat radius with a full payload. The combat radius is defined here as the distance that an aircraft could fly from its base to attack a target and still have enough fuel to return without aerial refueling. The total distance the aircraft would fly on such a mission would be twice that range. Missile ranges are simply the maximum distance from the launch location to the target.

The Current Long-Range Strike Force

Today's conventional long-range strike capability is provided by the Air Force's fleet of long-range bombers. The origins of the current bomber force go back to World War II, when large fleets of heavy and medium bombers were built to attack the industrial infrastructure of Germany and Japan and interdict surface forces and supplies moving to the combat zones. Shorter-range fighters were usually used to counter enemy fighters or to provide close air support to ground units.[4] Later, as part of the U.S. nuclear deterrent during the Cold War, bombers were designed with the long ranges and heavy payloads needed to carry large nuclear weapons from bases in the continental United States to targets deep within the Soviet Union. Although many strike fighters could also carry nuclear bombs, they were primarily designed for conventional warfare. Fighter-like aircraft were preferred for conventional missions because accurately delivering unguided conventional munitions against heavily defended tactical targets required low-altitude operations and fighter-like speed and agility. In that case, long range was less important because the fighters were expected to operate from bases in Western Europe, close to any fighting in a conventional war between the North Atlantic Treaty Organization and the Warsaw Pact.

At the height of the Cold War, the size of the U.S. bomber fleet was significantly larger than it is today. In 1963, there were 709 B-52s as well as more than 1,000 other bombers such as the B-47 and B-58. In addition to their long-range bombers, the Air Force and Navy had intermediate-range bombers—with payloads and range less than those of the heavy bombers—but by the early 1990s, the Air Force had retired its F-111s and the Navy had retired its A-6 Intruders.[5] Today, the bomber force numbers 182 aircraft, of which 96 are combat-ready (see Table 1-1 for a description of the quantities and capabili-

---

4. Although optimized for their given missions, heavy bombers, medium bombers, and fighter bombers could be used interchangeably if circumstances required and conditions permitted. For example, Navy fighter bombers were occasionally used to attack industrial targets on Japan's main islands, and the U.S. Eighth Air Force used heavy bombers to support the D-Day landings.

5. In terms of distance from the United States, short-range aircraft-carrier-based Navy strike fighters could be thought of as providing a long-range capability. Targets would still need to be relatively close to the sea, however.

Table 1-1.

Characteristics of Current U.S. Long-Range Bombers

	B-1B	B-2A	B-52H
Bomber Inventory			
Total active	67	21	94
Combat-ready	36	16	44
Average Age (Years)	17	11	43
Combat Radius[a] (Nautical miles)	1,800	2,000	3,000
Weight (Pounds)			
Empty	190,000	154,000	185,000
Maximum takeoff	477,000	337,000	488,000
Maximum Dropped Payload (Pounds)	54,000	34,000	Usually 50,000 [b]
Number of 2,000-Pound JDAMs	24	16	12 [c]
Crew	4	2	5
Employment Speed (Mach)	0.85 [d]	0.78	0.8
Stealth Features [e]	Some	Yes	No

Source: Congressional Budget Office based on Air Force briefings and data from the Congressional Research Service.

Note: JDAMs = Joint Direct Attack Munitions.

a. Measured on an unrefueled basis with a full combat payload.

b. The B-52 can deliver up to 65,000 pounds of payload when armed with conventional air-launched cruise missiles.

c. The number of JDAMs that the B-52 can carry is limited by the number of weapon stations that are able to provide target coordinates to the weapon before it is dropped.

d. The B-1 is capable of dashing at speeds up to about Mach 1.2 for limited distances.

e. Features designed to reduce the ability of defensive systems to detect or track the aircraft.

ties of aircraft in the current inventory).[6] The three types of bombers have significantly different characteristics that reflect the evolution of mission tactics and aeronautical technologies spanning the nearly four decades over which they were developed and fielded.

B-52H Stratofortress

The B-52 is the Air Force's oldest bomber. Between 1952 and 1962, the Boeing Company built 744 B-52s of various models. The "H" model in the current fleet first flew in 1961 and has more powerful engines, greater payload, and longer range than do earlier models. Today's fleet of

94 aircraft includes 44 that are combat-ready for both nuclear and conventional missions. B-52s are based at Barksdale Air Force Base in Louisiana and Minot Air Force Base in North Dakota.

Previous Air Force plans projected that B-52s would remain in the Air Force inventory until 2037, although the recently released 2006 QDR report states DoD's intention to reduce the B-52 inventory to 56 aircraft. Plans remain in place for maintaining and upgrading the smaller force. Planned upgrades to the B-52 include improvements to navigation systems, onboard computers, electronic countermeasures, and communications links. The Air Force has also considered replacing the engines with ones that have lower operating costs, although there are no current plans to do so. Continuing to operate the B-52s for another two to three decades could present problems with airframe life. Concerns have been voiced about

---

6. Aircraft might not be combat-ready for several reasons. For example, aircraft undergoing scheduled maintenance at a depot are not considered combat-ready. Similarly, the level of funding allocated for operating a type of aircraft also determines the number that can be kept combat-ready.

corrosion in the airframe and the fatigue life of the upper wing surface. As of May 2003, the average age of B-52s in the force measured in flight hours was around 15,860 hours, with the oldest having about 20,700 hours. DoD's Future Years Defense Program (FYDP) for fiscal years 2006 to 2011 includes about $1 billion for B-52 upgrades over that period. (That total does not include funds included to develop electronic warfare pods to enable using B-52s as standoff jammers against enemy air defenses. Those plans were dropped in the fiscal year 2007 budget request.)

The B-52 can carry more types of weapons than the B-1 or B-2 can—more than 20 different types of conventional and nuclear bombs and missiles from the current Air Force inventory. Weapons can be carried in the internal weapons bay or externally under the wings. Planned payload improvements include the installation of a laser targeting pod and the ability to carry new precision weapons as they are introduced into service. Although the airframe design does not incorporate stealth characteristics, the B-52 can attack targets with long-range cruise missiles, such as the Conventional Air-Launched Cruise Missile (CALCM), that enable it to remain beyond the reach of air defenses.

B-1B Lancer

After a controversial development history that included the cancellation of the –A model by the Carter Administration, the first B-1B bomber entered service in 1986. Rockwell International (now Boeing) produced a total of 100 aircraft by 1988. The current fleet size is 67 aircraft, with 36 that are combat-ready and configured for non-nuclear missions. The B-1 no longer has a nuclear mission. B-1s are currently based at Dyess Air Force Base in Texas and Ellsworth Air Force Base in South Dakota.

The Air Force's plans for the B-1, like those for the B-52, call for maintaining and upgrading the force until at least 2025. Upgrades include installation of improved defensive electronic countermeasures for better survivability and an improved computer system that would allow the aircraft to carry more types of precision weapons. In addition, the Air Force is improving communications links on the B-1B with the B-One Next Enhancement program, which seeks to integrate the Link-16 communications suite for jam-resistant communications as well as other equipment for beyond line-of-sight satellite communications. The 2006 FYDP included about $1.1 billion for B-1B upgrades over the 2006-2011 period.

The B-1 carries all its munitions in three internal weapons bays. The three-bay configuration gives the bomber the flexibility to carry a different type of munition in each. While the B-52 has a larger maximum payload in terms of weight, the B-1 can carry a greater number of most munition types (see Table 1-2). Although not considered to be a stealthy aircraft, the B-1 design incorporates features that give it a considerably lower radar signature than that of the B-52. In addition, the B-1 is the fastest of today's bombers and, with its afterburning engines, can dash at supersonic speeds for limited distances.

B-2A Spirit

The B-2 is the newest aircraft in the bomber fleet. Built by Northrop Grumman, the B-2 flew for the first time in 1989 and was declared operational in 1993. Only 21 aircraft were produced. The current fleet of 21 aircraft includes 16 that are combat-ready and are configured for both nuclear and conventional missions. The entire fleet is based at Whiteman Air Force Base in Missouri.

DoD also plans to maintain and upgrade the B-2 fleet until at least 2025. Planned improvements include changes to the radar, integration of new munitions, and changes to some of the stealth features to make the aircraft easier to maintain. DoD included about $1.9 billion for B-2 upgrades in its 2006-2011 FYDP.

Although the B-1 has some characteristics that reduce the ability of radars to detect and track it, the B-2 was designed around stealth to enable missions that could penetrate heavy Soviet air defenses. The primary focus on stealth came at the expense of other design attributes such as speed, payload, and maintainability. The B-2 is the smallest and slowest of today's Air Force bombers, and the need to maintain its radar-evading characteristics makes it difficult to deploy to forward bases unless special shelters are available. During Operation Enduring Freedom, B-2s flew missions to Afghanistan from the United States. Those missions required several aerial refuelings plus a brief stop at Diego Garcia to change crews. During Operation Iraqi Freedom, B-2s were based in special shelters on Diego Garcia to allow much-reduced mission times for the aircraft and their crews.

Capabilities for Future Long-Range Strike Systems

Although they are now used in conventional roles, today's bombers were originally designed to carry nuclear weap-

Table 1-2.

Maximum Number of Weapons Carried on Current U.S. Long-Range Bombers

Weapon	B-1B	B-2A	B-52H
Mk 82 Unguided 500-Pound Bomb	84	80	45
Mk 84 Unguided 2,000-Pound Bomb	24	16	18
CBU-87/97 Unguided Cluster Bomb	30	34	24
Wind-Corrected Munitions Dispenser	30	0	16
2,000-Pound Joint Direct Attack Munition	24	16	12
Joint Air-to-Surface Standoff Weapon	24	16	12
EGBU-28 Bunker Buster	0	8	0

Source: Congressional Budget Office based on data from the Air Force.

ons from bases in the United States to targets deep in the Soviet Union. They had to be large to achieve the long ranges and carry the large payloads necessary for that mission. For example, the distance from the B-52 base at Minot, North Dakota, to Moscow is more than 4,000 nm, a much longer distance than what would be anticipated for regional conflicts, and a cruise missile armed with a nuclear warhead weighs about 3,500 pounds, significantly more than the 2,000 pounds of a GBU-31 Joint Direct Attack Munition (JDAM), one of the heavier conventional munitions that is used in large numbers. The nuclear mission was also characterized by deliberate planning, operations from a well-equipped home base, and the need for only a few (or perhaps just one) nuclear attack sorties per aircraft.

For a new conventional long-range strike system, DoD could select an aircraft design with range and payload similar to those of today's bombers but with additional characteristics—such as ease of deployment to forward bases and ease of refueling and rearming for repeated missions—that are desirable in a conventional strike system. Large aircraft, however, have the disadvantage of high development, procurement, and operations costs.

Today's nonnuclear strike capability, measured in terms of JDAM-equivalent payload delivered per day without aerial refueling (which captures range, payload, and the number of sorties achievable per day), is heavily weighted toward fighters with much shorter ranges than those of heavy bombers (see Figure 1-1). Depending on the com-

bination of weapons and external fuel tanks carried, typical combat radii for U.S. strike fighters range from less than 350 nm to about 900 nm. Consequently, the bulk of U.S. strike capability is in that range. The figure shows that the delivery capacity of bombers at long ranges is about a quarter of the total delivery capacity of the Air Force at strike-fighter ranges.[7] Although the long range of heavy bombers is necessary for global missions such as those flown from the continental United States, a strike system with an intermediate range—greater than fighters' but less than heavy bombers'—might provide a less costly yet still very capable force. Other approaches might instead develop long-range missiles that could be launched from the ground or from ships or submarines.

Prior to the QDR, the Air Force had proposed a three-phase approach for improving long-range strike capabilities. For the near term, roughly from 2005 to 2015, that proposal called for continuing bomber upgrades such as those described above. For the mid-term, roughly from 2015 to 2020, the proposal called for fielding an interim system that, to the extent possible, used current technologies and avoided the risks of substantial development of advanced technology. The third phase called for fielding a highly advanced capability in about 2035 and beyond.

---

7. Aerial refueling increases the useful range of both fighters and bombers, although delivery capacity within a given period of time still drops with increasing mission distances because each mission takes more time.

Figure 1-1.

Potential Firepower of Current Air Force Strike Aircraft, Without Aerial Refueling

(Number of 2,000-pound JDAM-equivalents per day)

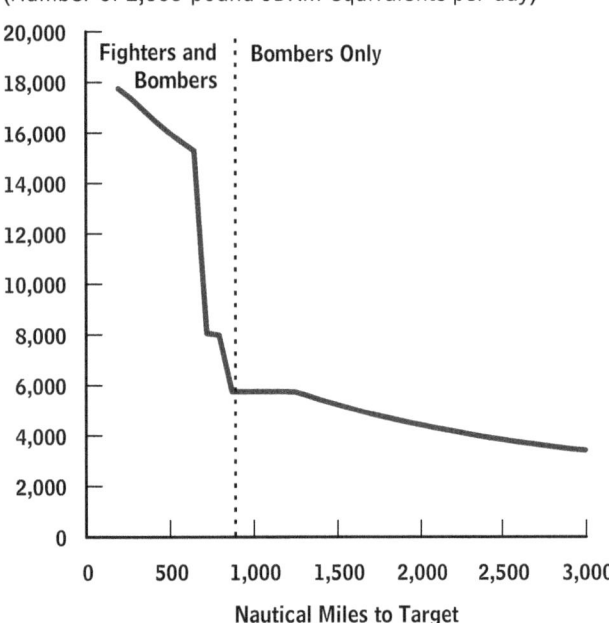

Source: Congressional Budget Office.

Notes: This figure is based on the Air Force's total inventory of aircraft. Numbers for operational aircraft would be lower.

JDAM = Joint Direct Attack Munition.

The QDR confirmed the need for continuing upgrades to existing bombers (Phase 1 of the Air Force plan) and called for fielding a new land-based long-range strike capability by 2018 (Phase 2 of the Air Force Plan) but did not describe that new capability as an "interim" one, leaving unaddressed the status of the third phase of the Air Force's proposal.

The general capabilities that the Air Force has proposed for future long-range strike systems include:

■ **Long Range:** the ability to attack targets anywhere on Earth.

■ **Responsiveness:** the ability to rapidly attack targets at any time under any conditions. Desired response times range from hours to minutes.

■ **Flexibility:** the ability to carry a wide variety of munition types and to easily incorporate new munitions or other new technologies.

■ **Survivability:** the ability to evade or defeat defenses in daylight as well as at night.

■ **Situational Awareness:** the ability to use onboard sensors plus connectivity to external information sources to improve combat effectiveness.

The Air Force has not identified specific systems to satisfy those objectives, although several systems such as a medium-range-bomber version of the F-22 fighter have been informally proposed.

Different performance characteristics can be incorporated into a strike system to achieve a given capability. For example, speed can be used to achieve survivability by reducing the amount of time the strike aircraft is within range of defenses. Alternatively, reducing the radar cross section could increase survivability by decreasing the range at which the aircraft would be detected. This study compares the capabilities of eight alternatives for future long-range strike systems and assesses how basic performance characteristics such as range, payload size and flexibility, signature, and speed contribute to a variety of desired capabilities similar to those identified by the Air Force. CBO used those basic performance characteristics to calculate design characteristics such as size, fuel load, airframe materials, and engine power. In turn, the development and procurement cost of each alternative was based on those design characteristics. Chapter 2 provides a detailed description of each CBO alternative and an estimate of its cost. Chapter 3 compares how well the alternatives provide the capabilities desired in a new long-range strike system. Details of the cost estimates are in the appendix.

Alternative Designs for Long-Range Strike Systems

The Congressional Budget Office considered eight alternative systems for conducting long-range strikes that span a range of performance and costs. The types of systems CBO analyzed would have performance characteristics (for example, range, speed, and payload) similar to systems that have been considered in recent studies prepared for the Department of Defense.[1] The next section describes the technical analyses that CBO used to estimate the general physical characteristics (for example, size and weight) of a system, given a set of desired performance characteristics. The subsequent section describes the physical characteristics for the specific systems CBO examined. Those physical characteristics, in turn, are necessary to make estimates of the costs to develop and purchase each system. The methods CBO used to develop cost estimates are described in the appendix.

The long-range strike alternatives CBO examined included five aircraft-based systems and three missile-based systems. The missile-based systems, which would use common aero vehicles to carry a warhead to the target, would be launched either from the ground on ballistic missiles or from satellites placed in advance in low-Earth orbit. After reentering the Earth's atmosphere, the CAVs would be able to glide to their target at hypersonic speed.

Technical Considerations for the Design of Long-Range Strike Platforms

The purpose of CBO's analysis is to demonstrate how military effectiveness and cost are related to key characteristics of long-range strike systems, particularly their range, payload, and speed. Considering both aircraft and CAVs, those key characteristics vary widely for the alternatives CBO analyzed. The speed of the alternatives varies from subsonic (for example, a C-17 arsenal aircraft that can cruise at about 76 percent of the speed of sound—Mach 0.76) to hypersonic (the long-range CAVs, which reenter the atmosphere at speeds exceeding Mach 20). The payloads carried by the long-range strike alternatives vary from 2,000 pounds for an individual CAV missile to about 134,000 pounds for the arsenal aircraft. The maximum range at which targets can be attacked varies from global (that is, the 10,000-nautical-mile—or more—range of the space-based CAVs) to 1,500 nm for the medium-range bombers and arsenal aircraft.[2] In addition, the takeoff and empty weights of the aircraft alternatives—which are directly related to their range, payload, and speed and are key determinants of cost—vary by about a factor of 5 (see Table 2-1).

Whether an aircraft flies at subsonic or supersonic speeds, the greater its range and payload, the heavier its weight at takeoff will be (to accommodate both the payload and needed fuel) and the higher its cost. The speed at which an aircraft flies also affects key aspects of its design and cost. For example, engines providing sufficient thrust for flight at supersonic speeds are generally less fuel-efficient and more costly than those designed to propel subsonic aircraft. The aerodynamic characteristics of supersonic aircraft are also different from subsonic aircraft, which is reflected in their differing shapes. Supersonic aircraft tend to be longer and narrower than subsonic aircraft in order to have an acceptable ratio of lift to drag; a narrow fuselage can, however, constrain the payload an aircraft can carry. Supersonic aircraft must also be constructed of materials that can withstand the increased friction-generated heat associated with supersonic flight, which also tends to

---

1. See, for example, Department of Defense, *Defense Planning Guidance: Long Range Global Precision Engagement Study Final Report* (April 2003).

2. Ranges of 3,000 to 4,000 nm are frequently quoted for the C-17 flying airlift missions. The 1,500-nm mission radius used here would correspond to a total unrefueled flight distance of 3,000 nm.

Table 2-1.

Long-Range Strike Alternatives Examined by CBO

	Unrefueled Range with Full Payload (Nautical miles)[a]	Speed (Mach)	Time Required to Strike a Target at Maximum Range (Hours)	Full Expended Payload (Pounds)	Empty Weight of Aircraft (Pounds)	Gross Takeoff Weight of Aircraft or Launch Weight of CAV (Pounds)
1 Arsenal Aircraft (C-17 with supersonic missiles)	1,500	0.76/3.0 [b]	3.4	134,000	277,000	569,509
2 Medium-Range Subsonic Bomber	1,500	0.85	3.1	20,000	60,000	120,000
3 Medium-Range Supersonic Dash Bomber	1,500	0.85/1.5 [c]	3.1	10,000	59,000	126,000
4 Long-Range Subsonic Bomber	2,500	0.85	5.1	40,000	128,000	283,165
5 Long-Range Supersonic Cruise Bomber	2,500	2.4	1.8	40,000	165,000	439,990
6 Medium-Range Surface-Based CAV	3,240	14	0.5	2,000	n.a.	48,000
7 Long-Range Surface-Based CAV	Global	20	1.1	4,000	n.a.	193,000
8 Space-Based CAV[d]	Nearly Global	20	1.1	16,000	n.a.	1,584,000

Source: Congressional Budget Office.

Note: CAV = common aero vehicle; n.a. = not applicable.

a.   The ranges shown are the maximum distance from an air base or launcher location to the target. For the aircraft alternatives, the total distance flown on an unrefueled mission would be double the values shown.

b.   The aircraft's speed is Mach 0.76; the missile's speed is Mach 3.0.

c.   The bomber's cruise speed to target is Mach 0.85; it can dash (with a reduction in range) at speeds up to Mach 1.5.

d.   The weights shown for space-based CAVs are for an eight-missile satellite. The launch weight includes the space-launch rocket used to put the satellite into orbit.

increase their cost. On the other hand, several of the long-range subsonic strike aircraft CBO considered were assumed to be stealthy (in particular, to be difficult to detect with radar), implying the use of radar-absorbing materials and construction techniques that also increase cost. (An aircraft's shape—for example, a tailless design—can also affect its stealth. Because of the associated heat environment, CBO assumed that for supersonic cruise aircraft, shape would be the primary means used to reduce radar signature.)

Range and payload also affect the costs of the CAV systems considered by CBO. A CAV contains a warhead made of conventional high explosives encased in a struc-ture designed to be able to maneuver and withstand the deceleration and heat generated by atmospheric friction as the CAV reenters the atmosphere at high speed and glides to its target. Generally, longer-range CAVs must be launched on trajectories that have them fly higher above the atmosphere, reenter at higher speeds, and experience higher deceleration than do shorter-range CAVs.[3] Providing the needed thermal protection and structure to withstand the forces associated with the deceleration affects cost. Additionally, costs are greater for the larger booster

---

3.   That general rule applies to the CAVs considered in CBO's analysis. Conceptual designs exist, however, for long-range CAVs that would fly on lower-altitude trajectories.

rockets needed to launch both longer-range CAVs and CAV systems with greater payloads (that is, simultaneous launch of a larger number of individual CAVs). The heaviest and most expensive launchers are those used to place multiple CAVs in low-Earth orbit.

The remainder of this chapter discusses in greater detail the design considerations incorporated in CBO's analysis of long-range strike alternatives.

Aircraft

CBO's analysis considers aircraft that could replace existing long-range heavy bombers (the B-52, B-1, and B-2) in terms of their range and payload, as well as aircraft that could provide improved responsiveness, measured by the time required to strike a target at maximum range. Because the Air Force has been discussing the possibility of pursuing a medium-range or "regional" bomber potentially derived from the F-22 fighter, CBO also considered three medium-range alternatives spanning a wide range of potential payloads. Needed range, payload, speed, and stealth determine the trade-offs that can be made among an aircraft's aerodynamics, propulsion, and structure.

Propulsion. All of the new aircraft examined use air-breathing turbine engines for propulsion. Performance of the propulsion system is typically measured by specific fuel consumption (SFC), which is the pounds of fuel consumed per hour per pound of thrust generated. Typical SFC values for jet engines range from 0.5 for an efficient turbofan to 1.0 or greater for high performance, but less efficient, supersonic aircraft engines. The lower the SFC, the less fuel consumed and the greater the aircraft's potential range or payload. According to CBO's calculations, aircraft that dash at supersonic speeds can have fuel consumption rates up to six or seven times higher than rates during subsonic cruise.

Aerodynamics. The shape of the wings and the fuselage of an aircraft determine how well it can maneuver through the air, as well as how much engine thrust is required to overcome the drag caused by the friction of air. One measure of aerodynamic performance is the ratio of the lift generated (which must be equal to the aircraft's weight in cruise) to the drag. The higher the lift-to-drag (L/D) ratio, the longer the range of the aircraft for a given speed and load of fuel. In addition, low-drag aircraft can cruise at higher speeds. Typical values of the L/D ratio for aircraft cruising at optimum speed (the speed that maximizes their range) vary from 10 to more than 20 for sub-

sonic aircraft; ratios of less than 10 are common for supersonic aircraft.[4]

Structures. The ratio of the empty weight of an aircraft—that is, its weight without fuel, crew, or payload—to its maximum takeoff weight indicates its capacity to carry fuel and payload. That ratio is called the empty weight fraction, which varies from 40 percent to 45 percent for bombers and cargo aircraft. The use of modern composite materials in aircraft construction can reduce the weight of an aircraft's structure while preserving needed strength. In general, for a given set of engines, the lighter the structure of an aircraft, the higher its cruise speed will be.

The effect that propulsion, aerodynamics, and structures have on an aircraft's range, speed, and payload can be quantified by the Breguet range equation, as follows:[5]

$$R = (V_c \,/\, SFC)(L/D)ln(W_o \,/\, W).$$

In the equation, R is the aircraft's range, V_c is the aircraft's cruise speed, SFC is the specific fuel consumption of the engines used on the aircraft, L/D is the aircraft's lift-to-drag ratio, W_o is the aircraft's gross takeoff weight, and W is the weight of the aircraft minus the fuel burned to reach the range R. Thus, the aircraft's range is determined by the performance of its propulsion systems $(V_c \,/\, SFC)$, its aerodynamics (L/D), and its structure $(W_o \,/\, W)$.[6]

Starting with a desired payload and assumptions regarding an aircraft's aerodynamics, propulsion, and structure, CBO used a model based on the Breguet range equation to estimate the gross takeoff and empty weights for the alternative aircraft displayed in Table 2-1. For the range estimates shown in the table, CBO assumed that the long-range strike aircraft would not be refueled during flight

---

4. Work has been done, however, on designs for supersonic aircraft incorporating features that could yield cruise lift-to-drag ratios approaching 10.

5. See, for example, Daniel P. Raymer, *Aircraft Design: A Conceptual Approach*, 3rd ed., American Institute of Aeronautics and Astronautics Educational Series (Reston, Va.: American Institute of Aeronautics and Astronautics, Inc., 1999).

6. For this formulation of the Breguet equation to be used, an aircraft's flight is divided into a number of phases—such as climb to altitude, cruise, and landing—during which SFC, velocity, and L/D are assumed not to vary (although they can be different for each phase). The formulation can also be adjusted to account for payload expended (that is, bombs dropped) during an aircraft's flight.

and would cruise until it reached the maximum range such that its remaining fuel would be sufficient to enable a safe return to its base. At that maximum range, the aircraft would drop its full payload of weapons and return to base, preserving about 10 percent of its full fuel load as a reserve in case of an emergency. Actual missions would be extendable if the aircraft was capable of aerial refueling. The total payload carried by an aircraft consists of the weapons it expends, any racks or other equipment needed to install the weapons in the aircraft, and the aircraft's crew and their equipment.

Other Design Considerations. CBO assumed that its alternatives for long-range strike aircraft would be manned. Unmanned versions of such aircraft have been proposed. The empty weights and costs of such unmanned aircraft might be less than those of the aircraft considered by CBO because unmanned aircraft do not need to carry crew support equipment. On the other hand, unmanned aircraft could require the use of high-bandwidth satellite communications for command and control and would require the development and testing of complex software automating their operation. Those factors would tend to increase the cost of unmanned aircraft relative to manned aircraft.

Common Aero Vehicles

For the foreseeable future, achieving very fast response times (that is, on the order of an hour or less) at global ranges will require systems such as CAVs that have trajectories through space. The CAVs CBO examined are reentry vehicles shaped to generate sufficient lift to glide many thousands of miles at hypersonic speed as they reenter the Earth's atmosphere. The CAVs would use a combination of thrusters and flaps to maneuver as they glide. CBO considered CAVs that could be launched at their targets using a surface-based intercontinental ballistic missile (ICBM) or a smaller surface-based medium-range missile, as well as CAVs that would be placed in equatorial low-Earth orbits (at an altitude of 270 nautical miles) and de-orbited when needed. Because CAVs have the ability to glide and maneuver in the atmosphere, they would be more costly and technically challenging than simpler reentry vehicles that might only be able to make minor course corrections as they reach the target. However, the CAVs' ability to shape trajectories means they

could avoid flying over diplomatically sensitive territory and could be launched on initial trajectories that would preclude spent booster rockets from falling on populated areas.[7]

The Defense Advanced Research Projects Agency was conducting a program known as FALCON (Force Application and Launch from the Continental United States) to develop the technology to enable CAVs to be built and made operational.[8] The CAV design that the FALCON program was considering would weigh about 2,000 pounds and carry a payload of 1,000 pounds—either a single conventional (that is, nonnuclear) warhead or multiple smaller munitions. The CAVs would be shaped to generate sufficient lift at hypersonic speeds to enable them to glide long distances downrange (that is, along the projection of their ballistic flight path) as well as maneuver to strike targets up to 2,500 to 3,000 nm crossrange (the distance perpendicular to their ballistic flight path). Their ability to glide and maneuver makes CAVs more technologically challenging than the reentry vehicles currently used to carry nuclear warheads, such as the Mark 12 launched on the Minuteman III ICBM. For example, to generate lift, the surface area of a CAV would need to be several times as large as that of an existing reentry vehicle—an area that must be protected from the heat generated during the prolonged flight of the CAV at hypersonic speeds. (A CAV would be in flight at hypersonic speeds for up to 30 times longer than the times for existing ballistic reentry vehicles. Some observers consider the development and testing of materials that could withstand the heat generated for that period of time to be the aspect of a CAV program incorporating the greatest technical risk.) The CAV's speed could give it an advantage

---

7. The Navy is exploring simpler maneuvering reentry vehicles with its Enhanced Effectiveness Initiative for Trident II ballistic missiles. See Congressional Research Service, *Conventional Warheads for Long-Range Ballistic Missiles: Background and Issues for Congress* (January 2006).

8. Although the FALCON program still exists, its focus has shifted from developing an operational weapon to more generic research into hypersonic flight. In this study, CBO used "common aero vehicle" as a generic term for such weapons because it is the most commonly known. The CAV is, however, a specific concept of the Air Force's and the Defense Advanced Research Projects Agency's. The Hypersonic Glide Vehicle is a related concept of the Army's.

over aircraft-delivered conventional munitions if it was used against hardened or deeply buried targets.[9]

The period spanning the time between the launch of a surface-based CAV and its arrival at a target comprises a number of phases. Those phases include the period during which the CAV is riding on its rocket launcher under thrust, the ballistic suborbital flight through space that occurs after the CAV separates from its launcher and lasts until the CAV reenters the atmosphere, and the period of hypersonic glide and maneuver through the atmosphere to a target. For long-range CAVs, the boost phase would last about three to four minutes, the suborbital phase would last about 30 minutes, and the glide phase would last from a few minutes (if little crossrange flight or additional downrange flight was required) up to 30 minutes. For medium-range surface-based CAVs, the boost phase would last somewhat more than two minutes, the suborbital phase would last several minutes, and the glide phase would be comparable with that of a long-range CAV.

The use of a space-based CAV would involve a set of phases having some commonality with surface-based CAVs but also with key elements that are different. In particular, a space-based CAV could not, in general, be fired immediately following a decision to attack a target. Because there would probably be a limited number of CAVs in orbit, a certain amount of time would elapse before some CAV's orbit carried it to a position in space within range of the target to be attacked. Once a CAV satellite was in position, the orbiting CAV would have to fire its attached retro-rocket to slow itself to suborbital speed and reenter the atmosphere. Finally, after reentry, the space-based CAV would glide and maneuver to its target in the same way as a surface-launched CAV would.

CBO determined the number of different orbital locations needed for the space-based CAVs and the size of their attached retro-rockets by imposing the requirement that the responsiveness of space-based and surface-launched long-range CAVs be equal (see Figure 2-1). CBO chose a retro-rocket providing a braking speed of

0.5 kilometers per second, corresponding to a de-orbit time of about 15 minutes from a 270-nautical-mile circular orbit.[10] Given a 15-minute de-orbit time, five orbital locations at the equator would provide the same responsiveness as would a long-range surface-launched CAV, assuming each CAV had the ability to glide and maneuver for up to 30 minutes within the atmosphere. (A constellation with more satellites in equatorial low-Earth orbit would provide only marginally shorter response times at greater cost.) The 2,500-to-3,000-nm crossrange flight that the CAVs could achieve would enable them to strike targets located in any of the world's major populated areas from an equatorial orbit.

Other choices for retro-rocket braking speeds are possible, with different braking speeds requiring a different number of satellites to achieve the chosen response time. However, there is no optimum choice of braking speed and number of satellites that would minimize the total mass (and, therefore, the launch costs) of a CAV satellite constellation for a fixed number of CAVs in orbit. A design with lower braking speeds would have lighter satellites because each retro-rocket would be smaller. However, to compensate for the increase in de-orbit time that would result from lower braking speeds, a greater number of those lighter satellites would be needed in orbit.

The Specific Long-Range Strike Alternatives CBO Examined

CBO analyzed eight alternative long-range strike systems that reflect several types of systems that have been proposed within the defense community:

Alternative 1—Arsenal Aircraft: Supersonic Missiles on C-17 Aircraft

A number of previous studies on long-range strike systems have examined the concept of an "arsenal aircraft" that could be a military cargo plane or commercial transport converted to carry large quantities of munitions.[11] That long-range strike aircraft would not be stealthy; so to provide it the capability to attack targets in the pres-

---

9. However, if the impact speed of a warhead is too great, its structure will be transformed from solid to fluid and it will fail to penetrate the target. Studies have shown that for steel impacts on granite and concrete, maximum penetration depths will occur for an impact speed of about 4,000 feet per second (or about Mach 4). See United States Air Force Scientific Advisory Board, *Why and Whither Hypersonics Research in the U.S. Air Force* (December 2000).

10. CBO chose a 270-nm altitude for the space-based CAVs because it is the lowest orbit that is high enough to prevent friction with the residual atmosphere that would cause the CAVs' orbits to decay substantially over their expected lifetime in orbit.

11. See, for example, Department of Defense, *Defense Planning Guidance: Long Range Global Precision Engagement Study Final Report* (April 2003).

Figure 2-1.

Response Times of Long-Range Common Aero Vehicles

(Minutes to strike target)

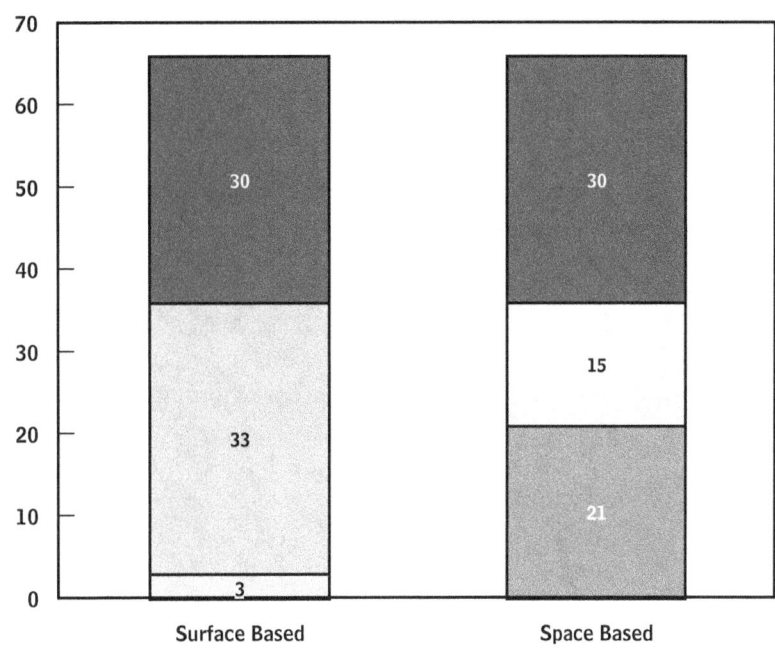
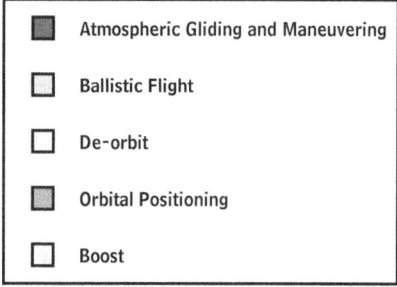

Source: Congressional Budget Office.

Notes: Response time for the space-based common aero vehicle assumes five satellites in equatorial orbit at an altitude of 270 nautical miles
and with a 0.5 kilometer per second de-orbiting rocket.

Atmospheric gliding and maneuvering time will vary depending on the target's location.

ence of sophisticated air defenses, CBO assumed that the
aircraft's payload would consist of high-speed cruise missiles with a speed of Mach 3 and a range of 500 nm.
Those high-speed missiles would be able to reach their
targets in about 20 minutes or less after launch, although
times on the order of several hours might be needed for
the aircraft to fly to the missile-launch location. CBO estimated that, consistent with the C-17's capabilities, the
arsenal aircraft would cruise at Mach 0.76 and carry a
payload of 167,000 pounds, about 80 percent of which
would be expendable munitions.[12] CBO's analysis indicates that the arsenal aircraft would have a combat range
of 1,500 nautical miles, which would enable it to attack
targets at a range of 2,000 nm with the addition of the
supersonic missile's 500-nm range.

---

12. The C-17's total payload is about 167,000 pounds. CBO assumed
that racks and dispenser mechanisms for the high-speed cruise
missiles carried by the aircraft would compose about 20 percent of
that total.

Alternative 2—Medium-Range Subsonic Stealth Bomber

As mentioned earlier, the Air Force has recently discussed
the potential need for a new medium-range bomber. In
this analysis, CBO examined a subsonic design having a
combat range of about 1,500 nautical miles without refueling, a payload of 20,000 pounds, and a cruising speed
of Mach 0.85. That design assumed a crew of two and
propulsion from two engines derived from existing designs. CBO's analysis indicates that the aircraft's empty
weight would be about 60,000 pounds, with a maximum
gross takeoff weight of 120,000 pounds. The design was
assumed to be highly stealthy, providing the capability to
conduct operations in the presence of sophisticated air
defenses.

Alternative 3—Medium-Range Stealth Bomber with Supersonic Dash

CBO also examined a medium-range bomber that would
cruise at subsonic speeds but that would have the capability to dash at supersonic speeds, hereafter referred to as

the medium-range supersonic bomber. That aircraft would be similar in concept to a medium-range bomber derived from the F-22 supersonic stealth fighter, which is being considered by the Air Force. The alternative examined by CBO would have a cruising speed of Mach 0.85 and could dash at speeds up to Mach 1.5 while carrying 10,000 pounds. If it cruised exclusively at subsonic speed, the aircraft's combat range would be 1,500 nautical miles. However, if the aircraft dashed to its target at Mach 1.5 and then returned at Mach 0.85, its combat range would be about 800 nautical miles; flying exclusively at Mach 1.5, its range would be somewhat less than 600 nautical miles. The aircraft would have a crew of two and be powered by two high-thrust engines, probably derivatives of the F119-100 engines used on the F-22. CBO's analysis indicates that the aircraft's empty weight would be about 59,000 pounds, and maximum gross takeoff weight would be about 126,000 pounds. The design was assumed to be highly stealthy.

Alternative 4—Long-Range Subsonic Stealth Bomber

When examining a design for a new long-range bomber, CBO considered what could be viewed conceptually as an improved version of the existing B-2. CBO assumed that such an aircraft would have a subsonic cruise speed of Mach 0.85, could carry 40,000 pounds of payload, and would have a combat range, without refueling, of 2,500 nautical miles (compared with about 2,000 nautical miles for a fully loaded B-2). CBO assumed that, as with the current B-2, this long-range strike aircraft would have a crew of two but would use two high-performance engines derived from current designs instead of the four engines used on the B-2. Assuming that the aircraft's design could incorporate improvements in both aerodynamic performance and engine fuel efficiency relative to the B-2, CBO's analysis indicates that the aircraft's empty weight could be about 128,000 pounds (compared with the B-2's 154,000 pounds) and that its gross takeoff weight would be about 283,000 pounds. The design would be highly stealthy.

Alternative 5—Long-Range Supersonic Cruise Bomber

CBO's analysis includes a bomber that could cruise at Mach 2.4 and carry a payload of 40,000 pounds. Assuming a maximum combat range of 2,500 nautical miles, CBO's analysis indicates that such an aircraft would have an empty weight of about 165,000 pounds and a gross

takeoff weight of about 440,000 pounds.[13] A supersonic bomber that could cruise to its target at Mach 2.4 would have responsiveness about 65 percent better than that of the long-range subsonic bomber considered by CBO (1.8 hours to reach a target 2,500 nautical miles away versus 5.1 hours). The aircraft would have two crew members and four (newly developed) engines. CBO assumed that the aircraft would be optimized for high-speed flight and would therefore have limited ability to loiter at subsonic speeds.[14] For this design, the aircraft's shape would be the primary means of achieving stealth—implying that the aircraft would be less stealthy than those in Alternatives 2, 3, and 4—because it is unclear to what extent the special materials used to help further reduce aircraft signatures would be robust enough to withstand the high temperatures of sustained supersonic flight.

Alternative 6—Medium-Range Surface-Based Common Aero Vehicle

On the basis of information provided by the Army, CBO assumed that a 2,000-pound CAV could be launched on a solid-fuel booster rocket small enough to be housed on a mobile launcher/erector. The booster could launch a single CAV on a trajectory with an apogee of about 49 nautical miles. Under CBO's assumptions, the CAV would be able to glide up to 3,200 nautical miles downrange and would have a maximum crossrange maneuvering capability of somewhat less than 950 nautical miles. CBO assumed that a medium-range CAV battery would include two missiles (each carrying a single CAV) placed

---

13. CBO's analysis assumed that technology available in the relatively near term would be used to build the Mach 2.4 long-range strike aircraft. Over the longer term, technology that might emerge from continuation of the Defense Advanced Research Project Agency's Quiet Supersonic Program (or related efforts) could make lighter-weight designs for long-range supersonic aircraft possible. If improvements in engine SFC and aerodynamics consistent with that program's goals were achieved, CBO's analysis indicates that a Mach 2.4 bomber with a 20,000-pound payload and a range of 2,500 nautical miles would have an empty weight of about 56,000 pounds. CBO did not consider alternatives for long-range strike aircraft that had cruising speeds well above Mach 3 (so-called hypersonic aircraft) because it assumed that the required advancements in technology could not be incorporated into an operational aircraft for more than 20 years.

14. There are proposals for variable-cycle supersonic engines with improved fuel efficiency at subsonic speeds. The designs for such engines introduce complexities in their operation and maintenance, however, and CBO did not assume that they would be developed for and used on the supersonic bomber considered in this analysis.

in two canisters carried on a single mobile launcher. Vehicles carrying launch control systems, command-and-control systems, and other support equipment would also be included in the CAV battery, which would be transportable by air. CBO assumed that 24 batteries would be purchased, 20 of which would be for operational use and four for spares.

Alternative 7—Long-Range Surface-Based Common Aero Vehicle

CBO assumed that long-range surface-launched CAV capability could be provided by 2,000-pound CAVs launched on Peacekeeper ICBMs being retired from their strategic nuclear mission. Two CAVs could be launched on a single Peacekeeper. CBO assumed that two sets of 10 Peacekeepers would be modified for operational use, with each set capable of launching 20 CAVs. One set would be placed in silos constructed at Cape Canaveral Air Force Station on the East Coast of the United States, and the second set would be placed at Vandenberg Air Force Base on the West Coast. That basing arrangement would enable targets to be attacked worldwide while precluding the impact of a spent Peacekeeper booster within a populated region (if used, the Peacekeepers would burn out over the Atlantic or Pacific Oceans). Four additional systems would be built as spares.

Alternative 8—Space-Based Common Aero Vehicle

CBO also considered an alternative that would base the 2,000-pound CAV in space. CBO assumed that five sets of eight CAVs would be placed in low-Earth orbit, with each set housed in a protective satellite providing power, thermal control, station-keeping (the ability to maintain proper orbital position and orientation), and communications for command and control. (The earlier discussion of general design considerations for CAVs provides the rationale for CBO's choices of orbit and number of satellites.) With eight CAVs housed in each of five orbiting protective satellites, this alternative would provide 40 operational CAVs, the same number assumed in Alternatives 6 and 7.[15] CBO assumed that the CAV satellites would have a service life of about 10 years in orbit. Maintaining a space-based CAV capability for 30 years, a period comparable with the typical service life of military

aircraft such as those considered in Alternatives 1 through 5, would require that enough CAV satellites be purchased to replace each one twice. With the addition of eight CAVs (and one protective satellite) as spares, a total of 128 CAVs would be purchased under Alternative 8.[16]

As in its analysis of potential designs for space-based interceptors used for missile defense, CBO examined two potential weights for the protective satellites: 50 percent of the weight of the CAVs to be housed and 20 percent of their weight.[17] CBO estimates that the total weight of each space-based CAV would be about 2,730 pounds: the CAV would weigh 2,000 pounds, and the solid fuel deorbit retro-rocket would weigh about 730 pounds. Therefore, eight CAVs housed in a heavier protective satellite would weigh about 32,760 pounds, and eight CAVs housed in a lighter-weight protective satellite would weigh about 26,200 pounds. CBO assumed that eight CAVs housed in a heavier protective satellite could be launched from Cape Canaveral into a 270-nautical-mile circular equatorial orbit using a heavy-payload version of the Delta IV Evolved Expendable Launch Vehicle (EELV).[18] A Delta IV medium-plus launcher should be capable of placing eight CAVs housed in a lighter-weight protective satellite in orbit.[19] CBO's cost estimates assume the heavier protective satellite and launch on a heavy EELV.

---

15. As mentioned previously, the crossrange maneuver capability of 2,500-to-3,000 nautical miles assumed by CBO would enable a CAV in an equatorial orbit to reach targets in North Korea or at higher latitudes. If development of CAVs with that crossrange capability proved infeasible, multiple sets of CAVs in multiple inclined orbits would be required to provide the ability to attack targets worldwide within an hour, substantially increasing costs.

16. The spare satellite would be needed if a launch vehicle failed during launch or if a satellite malfunctioned while in orbit.

17. That analysis is described in Congressional Budget Office, *Alternatives for Boost-Phase Missile Defense* (July 2004), available at www.cbo.gov.

18. See Boeing Corporation, *Delta IV Payload Planners Guide* (October 2000 and later supplements), available at www.boeing.com/defense-space/space/delta/docs/DELTA_IV_PPG_2000.PDF.

19. Ibid.

Comparing the Capabilities of the Long-Range Strike Alternatives CBO Examined

Two likely roles for future long-range strike systems will be to provide a new prompt, nonnuclear global strike capability and to contribute to the strike capabilities available to commanders in regional conflicts, especially those that are conducted over long distances because of local geography or basing restrictions. The Department of Defense, however, has not established future requirements for long-range strike systems with any detail beyond identifying general types of capabilities such as those described in the Secretary's Prompt Global Strike Plan and the Air Force's nascent three-phase plan for such systems (see Chapter 3).[1] *The Long Range Global Precision Engagement Study* prepared by the Air Force as directed by the *Fiscal Year 2004 Defense Planning Guidance* also established some initial structure to guide thinking about future long-range strike capabilities. The study defined four "capability focus areas" that describe what DoD expects future long-range strike systems to provide:

- *Prompt Global Strike*—the ability to strike anywhere (from very long ranges if necessary) within about 12 hours, with an emphasis on global access, survivability, and speed at the expense of volume of fire.

- *Prompt Theater Strike*—survivable strike capability over theater distances (up to 2,000 nautical miles) with a greater emphasis on volume of fire.

- *Persistent Area Strike*—strike capability for higher volume of fire from shorter ranges, and attacks against time-sensitive targets (10 to 15 minutes from an execute order) provided by high speed or long loiter times.

- *Battle Management, Command, Control, Communications, Computers, and Intelligence, Surveillance and Reconnaissance (BMC4ISR)*—a combination of onboard sensors and connectivity to external sensors and communications supporting the other three "focus areas."

To make quantitative comparisons of the military utility of different approaches for long-range strike systems, the Congressional Budget Office identified several specific capabilities that would enable a future system to contribute substantively to both prompt global strike missions and to air campaigns in regional conflicts. Those capabilities include:

- Reach—the ability to attack targets regardless of location.

- Responsiveness—the ability to attack targets quickly.

- Firepower—the ability to sustain attacks over time.

- Payload Flexibility—the ability to deliver different types of munitions.

- Survivability—the ability to avoid or defeat air defenses.

Those capabilities are related to, although not the same as, the *Long Range Global Precision Engagement Study*'s capability focus areas. CBO did not assess how much of a particular capability might be desired or needed but rather compared how well the postulated alternatives (as well as today's forces) could provide them. CBO assumed its alternatives would be designed to incorporate other attributes that have been identified as necessary for long-range strike, such as the ability to strike day or night and in poor weather, as well as connectivity to the networked

---

1. Office of the Secretary of Defense, *Report to Congress on: Prompt Global Strike Plan* (June 2005).

Figure 3-1.

Distribution of Worst-Case Penetration Distances for Countries of the World, Measured by Geographic or Operational Limits

(Cumulative percentage of countries)

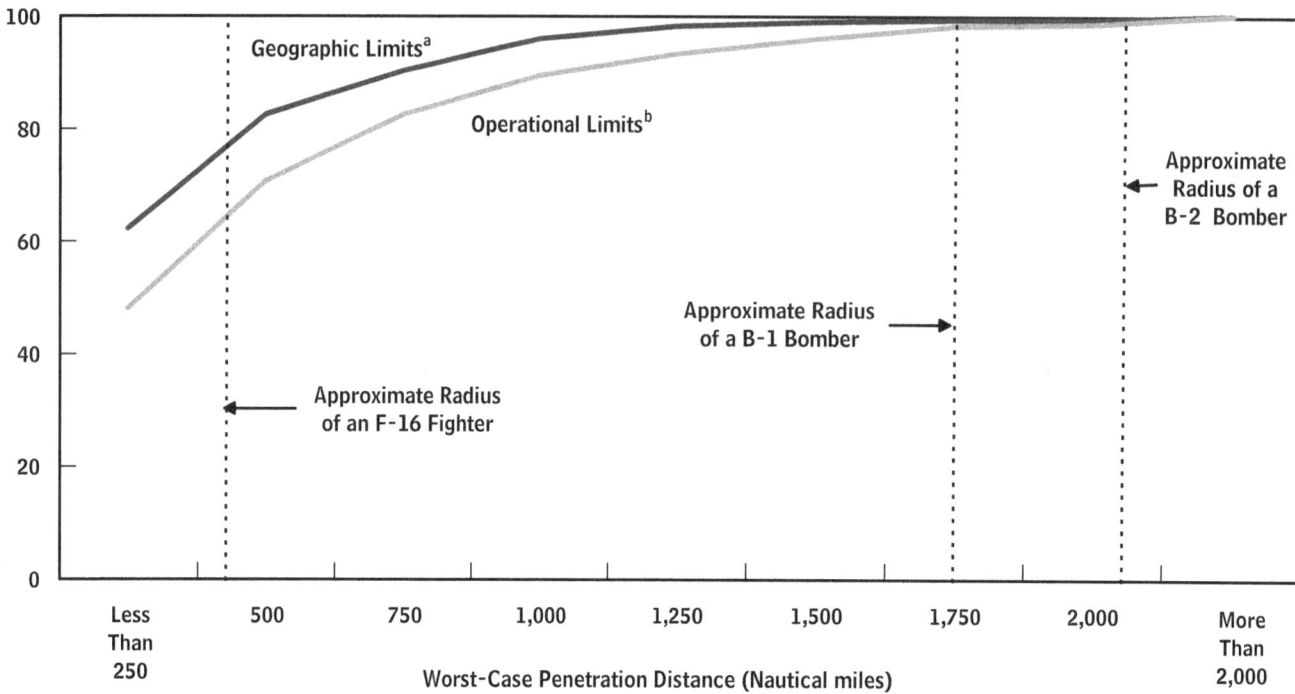

Source: Congressional Budget Office based on data from the Central Intelligence Agency, *World Fact Book* (2003), and the Air Force.

Note: Radius of a B-52 bomber is approximately 3,000 nautical miles.

a. Geographic limits are based on a country's long axis or maximum distance from open ocean.

b. Operational limits are based on geographic limits plus the need for a tanker to stand off 100 nautical miles and a 30 percent range penalty to account for threat avoidance.

force (for example, the ability to send and receive targeting information).

Ability to Reach Targets Anywhere on Earth

With the exception of Alternative 6—the medium-range common aero vehicle—all of CBO's long-range strike alternatives offer sufficient range or endurance to fly from any base or launch location to almost any other point on Earth. Long-range CAVs (Alternative 7) and space-based CAVs (Alternative 8) could do so unassisted, and the aircraft alternatives could do so with aerial refueling support. Operational restrictions, however, can prevent a system from being able to attack a target that it would otherwise be physically able to reach. For example, because vulnerability to air defenses usually prevents air-

borne tanker operations inside denied or hostile airspace, aerial refueling may not be available in all cases where it might be needed to allow strike aircraft to attack targets deep within a large country's borders.[2]

In general, the longer the unrefueled range of a system is, the greater its flexibility to attack targets wherever needed. To quantify the flexibility offered by increasing unrefueled range, CBO estimated what fraction of the

2. Today's tanker fleet comprises converted commercial airliners that are easily detected by radar, and the task of aerial refueling requires the tanker and the receiver to fly a predictable (and easy-to-target) profile while fuel is being transferred. Consequently, most refueling is done in secure airspace, although tankers can be sent into hostile airspace if the need warrants it. There have been proposals to develop stealthy tankers, but the feasibility of achieving a stealthy refueling capability is undetermined.

Figure 3-2.

Ability of Alternative Strike Systems to Attack Targets Deep in Enemy Territory

(Percentage of countries in the world covered)

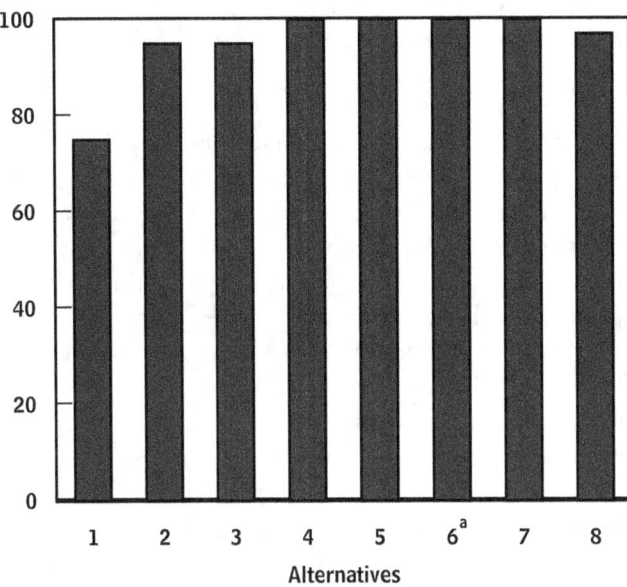

Source: Congressional Budget Office.

Note: Alternative 1 = Arsenal aircraft
Alternative 2 = Medium-range subsonic bomber
Alternative 3 = Medium-range supersonic dash bomber
Alternative 4 = Long-range subsonic bomber
Alternative 5 = Long-range supersonic cruise bomber
Alternative 6 = Medium-range surface-based common aero vehicle
Alternative 7 = Long-range surface-based common aero vehicle
Alternative 8 = Space-based common aero vehicle

a.   The results for the medium-range common aero vehicle in Alternative 6 assume that the launcher can be located near the target country.

world's countries would be entirely accessible to each long-range strike alternative. That entailed comparing an alternative's unrefueled range (in the case of the penetrating-aircraft alternatives) or its missile range (in the case of the arsenal-aircraft and the CAV alternatives) with the geographic dimensions of each country. To provide full coverage, CBO assumed that the necessary penetration distance for each country would be the smaller of the longest distance between two points within a country's borders or the farthest distance from an ocean (because strike aircraft could approach from the sea). By that measure, even shorter-range tactical fighters could reach any point in most of the world's countries (see Figure 3-1).

For example, an F-16 carrying two 2,000-pound Joint Direct Attack Munitions could reach any point within about 80 percent of the world's countries if aerial refueling was available at the target country's border (and along the route to the border, if necessary) and if its route between the tanker and the target was a straight line.[3] The F-16's coverage would drop to about 65 percent of all countries if additional operational considerations—in this example, the need for a tanker to stand off 100 nm outside of the adversary's border and a 30 percent range penalty to account for indirect routes to avoid air defenses—are included. (This discussion does not address whether the strike system could successfully avoid air defenses. Survivability is examined in a later section.) Today's heavy bombers offer full coverage, even with the example's operational constraints (as shown in Figure 3-1).

Most of CBO's long-range strike alternatives offer complete or nearly complete coverage as well (see Figure 3-2). The long-range surface-based CAV and the two long-range-bomber alternatives would fully cover all countries, and the two medium-range-bomber alternatives would fully cover about 95 percent of all countries. The medium-range-bomber alternatives would achieve full coverage if they were allowed to enter enemy airspace from points on the border closer to the target. The space-based-CAV alternative's crossrange maneuverability—the ability to fly north or south from its equatorial orbit—would limit its coverage to North or South latitudes less than about 60 degrees but allow it to still fully cover about 97 percent of the world's countries. The medium-range-CAV alternative would offer full coverage if its launcher could be positioned close enough to the target country—no farther than about 500 nm for worst-case geography and the largest countries but as far as 2,000 nm in most cases. Consequently, medium-range CAVs carried on board surface ships or submarines would offer good coverage. (CBO did not estimate the costs of putting CAVs aboard ships or submarines.)

The arsenal aircraft would offer the least coverage among CBO's alternatives. Its 500-nm missile range and the inability of C-17s to penetrate air defenses would limit its coverage to around 75 percent of the world's countries. (CBO assumed that the C-17 would operate 100 nm from the border but that the missile would fly directly to

---

3.   The percentages cited are based on a list of countries found in Central Intelligence Agency, *World Fact Book* (2003). They include all countries or autonomous areas listed.

its target.) That percentage would improve if the C-17 could launch its missiles from a more favorable location on the perimeter of the target country or if air defenses were suppressed enough to allow the C-17 itself to penetrate the target country's borders.

This geography-based approach to examining the penetration capability of CBO's alternatives does not distinguish among nations that are more or less likely to be considered potential threats. Those judgments are subjective and change over time. For three nations commonly mentioned today as current or possible future adversaries—North Korea, Iran, and China—the CAV and long-range-bomber alternatives would provide total coverage. The medium-range bombers could not reach parts of China, and the supersonic air-launched missile could not reach parts of Iran and China.

Responsiveness

Responsiveness in a long-range strike system is the ability to quickly attack a target after the order to do so is given. Systems that can execute their attacks in a shorter period of time are said to be more responsive than those needing more time.

In its analysis, CBO considered two operational contexts for assessing responsiveness:

- *Preplanned Missions*—those for which the identity of the target is known before the mission begins. Preplanned missions typically achieve responsiveness on a timescale of hours or days.

- *Fleeting Target/Ground Support Missions*—those for which the specific target is not known before the mission begins, such as missions involving close air support targets identified by ground controllers when the aircraft are already overhead. Such missions typically aim for responsiveness on the order of a few minutes.

Those two types of responsiveness are examined separately because each would require that strike systems be employed differently.

Many strike missions are preplanned and can be prepared long in advance of the actual attack or rapidly as a conflict progresses. Examples of preplanned missions that were prepared rapidly were seen at the beginning of Operation Iraqi Freedom when the initial air strikes were advanced several hours in an attempt to hit leadership targets that intelligence sources were thought to have located. Responsiveness to fleeting targets was illustrated later when a B-1B bomber over Iraq was diverted to attack a building where Saddam Hussein was thought to be located. The bomber struck the target less than 15 minutes after receiving the order to attack.

The responsiveness needed against a target depends on what the target is and what the target is doing. For example, high responsiveness would usually be desired against an adversary's mobile ballistic missile launchers because they might launch their missiles at any time and because they are difficult to track for long periods of time. The responsiveness desired against an armored unit, on the other hand, would depend on what that unit was doing. If it was far from friendly forces, responsiveness on the order of hours or even days might be sufficient because the unit would pose no immediate threat and would be easy to track. (It might not even be deemed worth an attack.) If the same unit was about to overrun friendly ground forces, however, responsiveness on the order of minutes would be needed.

Several steps contribute to the time that elapses between when a target is detected and when it is attacked. Those steps include time for transmission and processing of data from the sensor that detects the target, time for analyzing the data and deciding to attack, time for the decision to reach the unit that will conduct the attack, and time to prepare and execute the mission. Total times can vary widely depending on factors such as the political or military situation, the type of target, the volume of data being processed, and the type of strike system tasked to perform the attack. This analysis focuses on the time that would elapse between when a strike order is received by the attacking unit and when weapons hit the target.

Responsiveness in Preplanned Attacks

Responsiveness in preplanned attacks is primarily a function of the speed of the strike system and the distance to the target. Thus, higher speeds and the ability to be based close to potential targets contribute significantly to a strike system's responsiveness.[4] The benefit of higher

---

4. Other contributing factors include the ability to be quickly launched after an attack order is received and the ability to rapidly plan the mission (or to conduct detailed planning during transit to the target). CBO assumed that its alternatives would be designed to incorporate those characteristics.

Figure 3-3.

Response Times of Alternative Strike Systems for Preplanned Missions

(Hours to strike target)

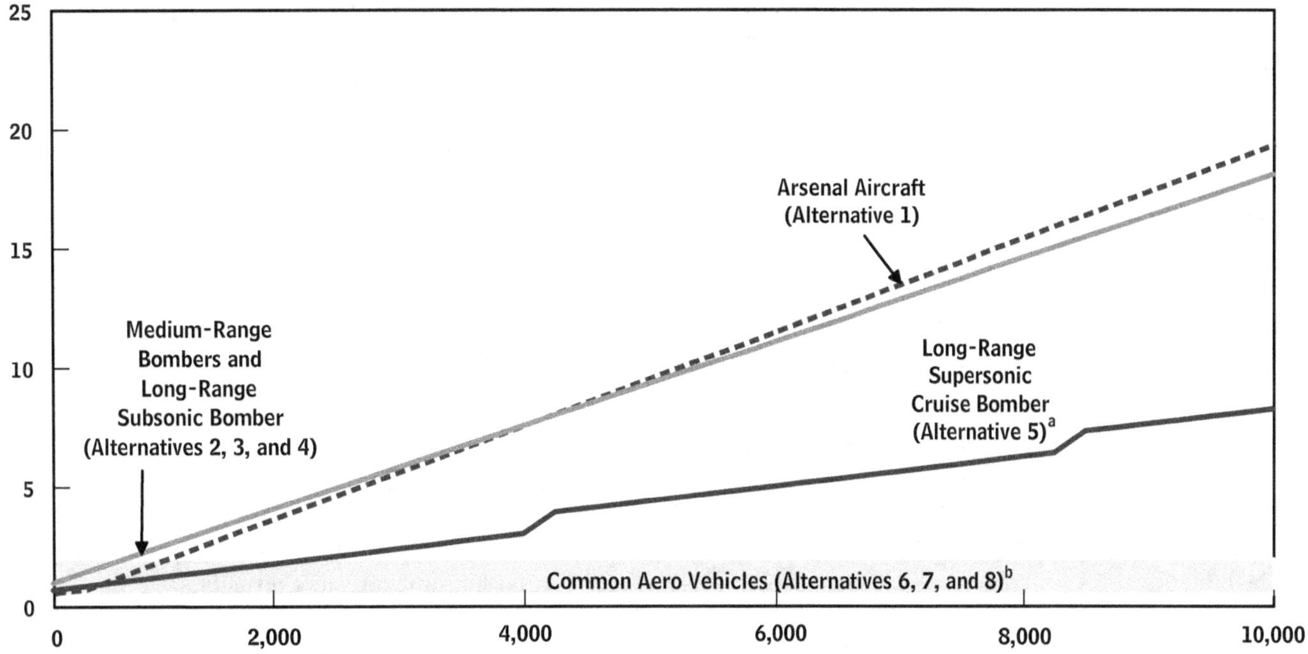

Source: Congressional Budget Office.

a.   The steps in the line for the supersonic cruise bomber result from its need to slow for aerial refueling.

b.   Response times for the common aero vehicle alternatives will vary for a given distance to the target, depending on the specific flight
profile needed. The medium-range common aero vehicle has a maximum distance to target of 3,200 nautical miles.

speed, however, depends on the distance to be traveled, because over longer distances, a faster system has more time to pull ahead of a slower system. To capture that dependence, CBO compared the preplanned mission responsiveness of its long-range strike alternatives over different mission distances (see Figure 3-3).

Over global distances, the CAV alternatives offer by far the best response times because they travel at speeds many times faster than aircraft do. The response times for CAVs are shown as a band because those times do not depend only on the distance between launch point and target. The specific flight times are dependent on the trajectory that must be flown and are therefore influenced by other factors such as the amount of glide trajectory relative to ballistic trajectory needed and, in the case of Alternative 8, the locations of the space-based CAVs in orbit at the time a launch order is received.[5] Shots requiring a crossrange trajectory would need the longer times because the difference in range off the ballistic trajectory would be achieved by CAV maneuvers in the atmosphere. For the

space-based CAV, those times could vary from about 15 minutes to one hour depending on the delay needed for an orbiting CAV satellite to move into position and the amount of maneuvering the CAV would require after it reentered the atmosphere. The upper bound of responsiveness for the space-based CAVs could be reduced by placing more CAVs in orbit because that would reduce the wait for a CAV to reach the correct orbital position. Response times could vary from about 30 minutes to one hour for the long-range surface-based CAV. The medium-range CAV could offer faster response times at shorter ranges because of its shorter ballistic phase of flight. Short response times for the medium-range CAV assume that the launcher is within range of the target. The response time could be many hours or days if

5.   Although ranges for the CAV options are referred to in terms of ground distance between the launcher and the target, CAVs would actually fly a much longer distance along their suborbital trajectories. Similarly, the actual distance flown by the space-based CAVs would include the vertical distance from orbit.

Table 3-1.

Flight Time Needed to Reach a Target in Afghanistan

		Time to Target (Hours)	
Launch Location	Type of Base	Flying at Mach 0.85[a]	Flying at Mach 2.4[b]
United States	U.S. territory	15.0	6.0
Guam	U.S. territory	10.0	4.0
Diego Garcia	Territory of an ally	6.0	2.2
Indian Ocean	Aircraft carrier	2.5	c

Source: Congressional Budget Office.

Notes: Diego Garcia is a British-held island in the Indian Ocean.

Aerial refueling would be necessary for the notional missions presented in this table.

a. A speed of Mach 0.85 is representative of the aircraft in Alternatives 2, 3, and 4 and today's bombers or fighters.

b. A speed of Mach 2.4 is representative of the aircraft in Alternative 5.

c. With foreseeable technology, a Mach 2.4 cruise bomber would probably be too large to operate from an aircraft carrier.

launchers must first be moved to a location within range of the target.

The response times for the aircraft alternatives are a strong function of speed. The three subsonic aircraft alternatives (1, 2, and 4) have similar response times over a wide band of ranges because their speeds are about the same over most of their flight to the target. The arsenal aircraft is slightly less responsive because the C-17 aircraft is slower than the penetrating bombers, at Mach 0.76 versus Mach 0.85, although the supersonic missile would fly the final 500 nm of its mission at Mach 3. The response time of Alternative 3 would be similar to that of the subsonic-only aircraft because it could dash at speeds up to Mach 1.5 only for limited distances. Its range would be less than 1,000 nm if it cruised at supersonic speeds. The supersonic cruise bomber (Alternative 5) offers a considerably quicker response, although it would have to slow for refueling during missions over distances longer than its unrefueled radius (a consideration that results in the stair-step shape of the line in Figure 3-3 on page 19).[6] The response-time advantage for Alternative 5 increases with mission distance. Over long regional conflicts—distances of about 1,000 nm to 1,500 nm—the response time of the supersonic cruise bomber would be one to two hours shorter than the time for the subsonic alternatives. For global missions, the response time for Al-

ternative 5 would be about eight hours shorter than the time for the subsonic-aircraft alternatives.

None of today's systems could match the responsiveness of the CAV alternatives over long ranges. Only airborne aircraft loitering in the area (or, possibly, aircraft on alert at a base very close to the target) could do so. Today's subsonic bombers would provide ranges and response times similar to those of CBO's subsonic-aircraft alternatives if they were flying over similar distances. Navy aircraft have the potential to offer better response times than those of the aircraft alternatives examined by CBO if an aircraft carrier was in the area (see Table 3-1). For example, a strike aircraft from a carrier in the Indian Ocean could have similar responsiveness against a target in Afghanistan to that of the Mach 2.4 bomber in Alternative 5 based on the island of Diego Garcia. However, arranging tanker support for the shorter-range Navy aircraft might not be possible on such short timelines. A carrier-based aircraft with a range like that of the medium-range-bomber alternatives would not need such support, however. Operating from a carrier would have the advantage of obviating permission to use foreign bases but would still require that a carrier be in the area.

Responsiveness Against Fleeting Targets

Although the preplanned response times estimated above are adequate against many types of targets, they are too long for others. Highly time-sensitive targets include those that pose an immediate danger to friendly forces or

---

6. The subsonic bombers might also slow to refuel, but the difference in speed would be much smaller.

civilians, those that are exposed for only brief periods of time, and those on the move if they cannot be reliably tracked. Inadequate responsiveness can lead to unsuccessful attacks because:

■ The target is able to complete its hostile action before the strike is conducted (for example, an enemy unit destroys a friendly unit before close air support arrives);

■ Unbeknownst to intelligence, surveillance, or reconnaissance (ISR) systems, the target moves before the strike is conducted (for example, a terrorist leader leaves a safe house before a strike delivers its attack on a now-vacated building); or

■ The target moves and the strike system cannot locate it to complete the attack (for example, a mobile missile launcher is several miles from its anticipated location before the strike arrives).

For time-sensitive targets, the probability of successfully attacking decreases as response time increases. In the first two examples above, as time passes, the probability that the target will either be relevant or present decreases with time. In the third example, the target may still be in the general area, but the strike system might have to search for it because the target's movement creates uncertainty as to where it will be relative to its last known location. When there is great uncertainty about the target's location, the strike system must be able to search the area with its own sensors, a potentially time-consuming process that could expose the attacker to air defenses.

The very short response times needed against fleeting targets—the *Long Range Global Precision Strike Study* set a goal of five to 10 minutes from an execute order—can be achieved only with very high speeds or with systems that are close to the target from the outset.[7] Aircraft would almost certainly have to be airborne before receiving the mission because the time needed to taxi and take off could consume much of the available time. For example, during Operation Desert Storm, the Air Force maintained combat air patrols of strike aircraft, usually F-15Es, over Iraq in order to rapidly attack mobile SCUD

missile launchers. Those aircraft could be minutes away if a launch or launcher was detected—close enough to find and hit it before it could return to hiding. By comparison, aircraft waiting on the ground would have taken at least an hour to reach the area—not soon enough to catch the launchers that returned to hiding shortly after firing their missiles.

In contrast to preplanned missions originating at air bases, aircraft-based strike systems can have shorter response times than those for the CAV alternatives when they operate from airborne orbits. If air defenses have been suppressed, aircraft could be placed in orbits close to or over areas where targets might be expected to appear. If air defenses have not been suppressed, orbits could be located in the nearest secure airspace. Because the precise locations of targets are not known in advance—if they were, they would be preplanned targets—planners must provide enough orbits so that a strike aircraft is always close enough to provide a sufficiently short response time. Consequently, a primary disadvantage to loitering orbits is the large number of aircraft that might be needed to maintain them: aircraft that could be used elsewhere end up tasked to perform orbits in the hope that targets will reveal themselves.

In general, more effective loitering strike systems will require fewer aircraft to cover a given target area with a desired response time. Both speed and endurance can help reduce the number of strike systems needed to provide short response times over a target area. Higher speed enables greater area coverage from an orbit, and longer endurance means fewer systems are needed to maintain an orbit around the clock.

The arsenal aircraft (Alternative 1) would have a significantly greater area of coverage from a single orbit than would the other aircraft alternatives because the supersonic missile could fly up to 500 nm to the target at Mach 3, faster than the other aircraft alternatives (see Figure 3-4). Area coverage would increase slowly for targets that were more than 500 nm from the arsenal aircraft because the C-17 must fly toward the target at Mach 0.76 before firing the Mach 3 missile. (That causes the sudden decrease in the slope of the curve for Alternative 1 in the figure.)

The subsonic penetrating-bomber alternatives (2 and 4) would have the smallest area of coverage because of their low speed, although that coverage would increase if, as

---

7. Improvements in ISR systems and communications links to strike platforms could also help responsiveness. For that reason, good connectivity to the ISR and communications networks is stressed as an important attribute for future long-range strike systems.

Figure 3-4.

Area Covered from Loitering Orbit for Different Response Times

(Thousands of square nautical miles)

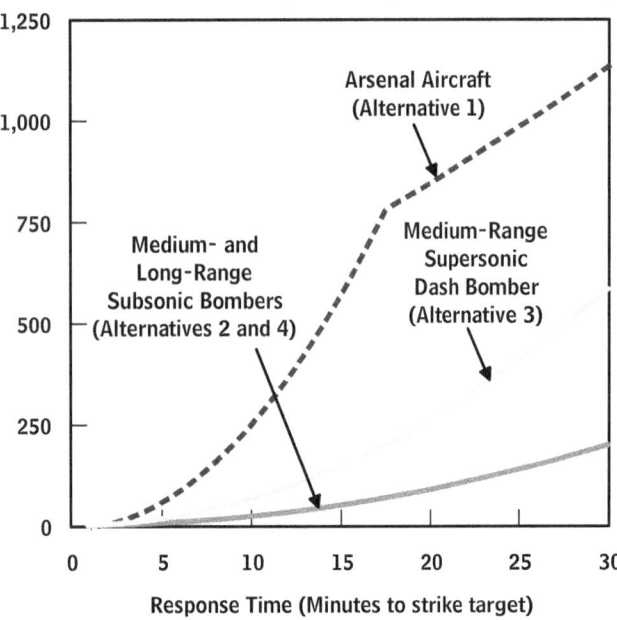

Source: Congressional Budget Office.

with the arsenal aircraft, they could be armed with high-speed missiles. The medium-range supersonic bomber would perform better than the subsonic alternatives, although it would lack the fuel for a Mach 1.5 dash to ranges much greater than the supersonic missile could cover at Mach 3. The higher-speed long-range supersonic bomber (Alternative 5)—not shown in the figure—would probably not be employed in this type of mission. Its design would probably not be suitable for the long periods of efficient low-speed flight needed for a loiter mission. (Its endurance would be similar to that of the aircraft in Alternative 4 in terms of distance flown but much shorter in terms of time aloft.)

The picture changes somewhat when endurance is factored into the number of aircraft required to continuously cover a given area (see Figure 3-5). The figure shows the number of strike aircraft needed to continuously cover 45,000 square nautical miles (about 25 percent of Afghanistan) with a response time of not longer than 10 minutes. Despite having less endurance than some of the other alternatives, the large area covered by the supersonic missiles enables the arsenal aircraft to provide coverage with fewer orbit locations than the other al-

ternatives could—and thus fewer total aircraft—for orbit locations up to 1,000 nm from base.[8] The number of aircraft needed to fill an orbit increases rapidly as the transit distance to the orbit approaches the range of the aircraft because the time on-station for each aircraft is rapidly shortened. Beyond a 1,000-nm transit distance, only the long-range subsonic bomber is well short of its maximum range (2,500 nm versus 1,500 nm for the other alternatives). Consequently, if orbit locations are farther than 1,000 nm from a base (or last aerial refueling), long-range subsonic bombers can provide 10-minute response times with the fewest number of aircraft dedicated to filling the orbits. The medium-range bombers require the largest number of aircraft because they have neither the highest speed nor the longest endurance. The faster medium-range bomber, in Alternative 3, can provide coverage with fewer aircraft than Alternative 2 can because its higher dash speed allows it to cover a greater area from each orbit.[9]

The preceding analysis assumes that a bomber's payload is fully expended before it returns to base. That would be the case if targets were to arise at a rate that would use up the bomber's munitions during its time on-station or if the bombers were tasked to strike preplanned targets at the end of that time. If it was necessary to bring back unexpended weapons or if weapons were expended before the available fuel, loiter times would be shorter.

Although the CAV alternatives could provide full and continuous coverage from a single location—a country or ship in the region for Alternative 6, the United States for Alternative 7, or low-Earth orbit for Alternative 8—their responsiveness would be limited by the time required to fly their trajectories. At best, that time would be on the order of 10 minutes for a medium-range CAV if the warhead required minimal glide and maneuver time in the atmosphere—that is, if the launcher was relatively close to the target. The space-based CAV would need at least

---

8.   Distances shown in the figure are from a ground base. Coverage could also be measured relative to the distance from an aerial refueling orbit. Relative results would be similar.

9.   The figure shows Alternative 3 requiring more aircraft than Alternative 2 for orbits greater than about 1,000 nm from a base. That occurs because at long ranges, the supersonic dash that gives the bomber in Alternative 3 its extra reach would also seriously limit orbit time because of the extra fuel consumed during the dash. Because orbiting tactics would probably require air superiority, tankers might be on hand to mitigate that limitation.

Figure 3-5.

Number of Aircraft Needed for 24-Hour Coverage of 25 Percent of Afghanistan with a 10-Minute Response Time

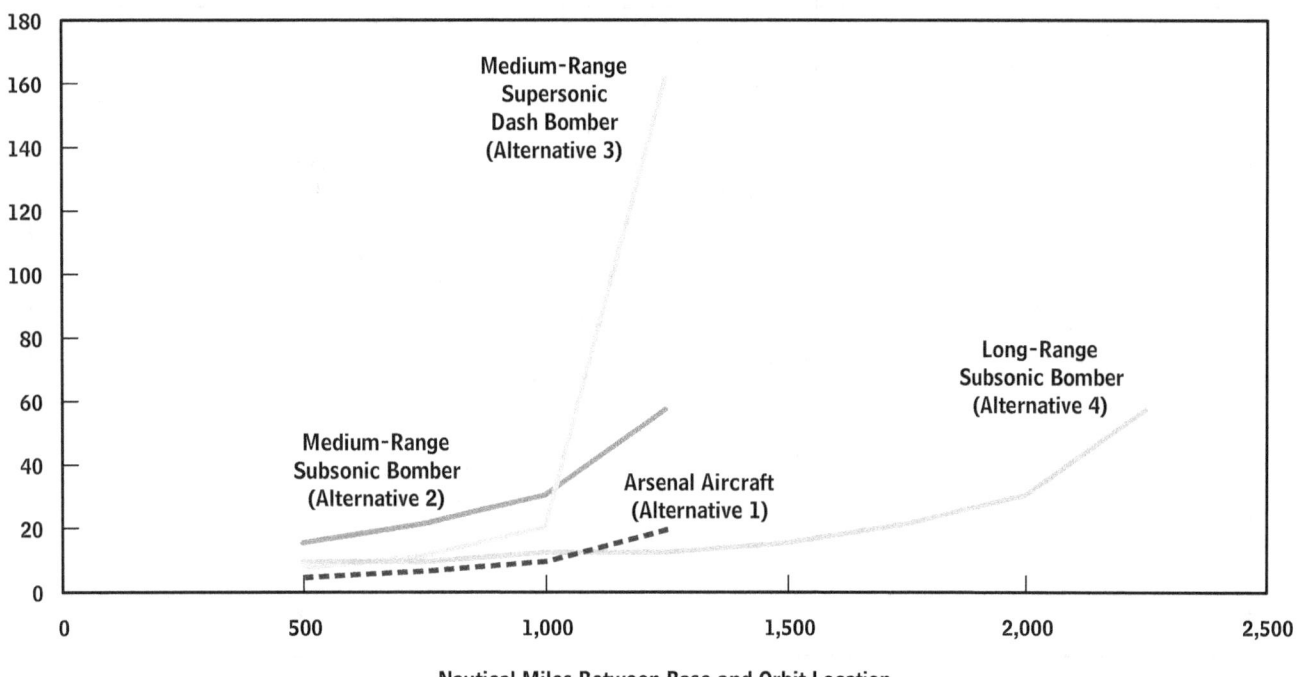

Nautical Miles Between Base and Orbit Location

Source: Congressional Budget Office.

Note: This figure assumes that an aircraft expends all of its munitions before returning to base. Endurance would be lower (that is, more air-craft would be needed) if an aircraft returned with unused munitions. Endurance would be higher (fewer aircraft would be needed) if distance was measured from an airborne tanker rather than from a ground base.

15 minutes to de-orbit, and the surfaced-based CAV would need at least 30 minutes to fly from the United States. If significant glide time in the atmosphere was needed, response times could be as high as half an hour for the medium-range CAV alternative or about an hour for the other CAV alternatives.

Sustained Firepower

The previous discussion focused on achieving very rapid attacks against high-value targets that are likely to be present in limited numbers. Long-range strike systems can also be important contributors to large-volume attack operations such as those seen in major theater wars. They can be especially important if the availability of bases near the conflict is limited.

A system's sustained firepower is determined by the amount of munitions it can deliver per mission and its sortie rate—the number of missions it can fly per day.

The sortie rate for an aircraft depends on the duration of the missions to be flown and on "turn time," the time needed between missions for servicing and rearming. CBO assumed that all of the aircraft would be designed for quick turn times but that larger and faster aircraft would need longer turn times because they carry a larger number of munitions and larger fuel loads.

Under the alternatives considered here, CAVs would be incapable of providing sustained firepower because they would probably be purchased in limited numbers and because each CAV could be used only once. Among the other alternatives, the two medium-range bombers offer the lowest bomb delivery rate because they have smaller payloads than the longer-range alternatives and fly at sub-sonic speeds (see Figure 3-6). The aircraft in Alternative 3 can dash for short distances at Mach 1.5 but would prob-ably not fly entire missions at its dash speed. The arsenal aircraft and long-range penetrating bombers have pay-loads higher than those of the medium-range bombers

Figure 3-6.

Bomb Delivery Rates for Alternative Strike Aircraft

(Number of 2,000-pound JDAM-equivalents per aircraft per day)

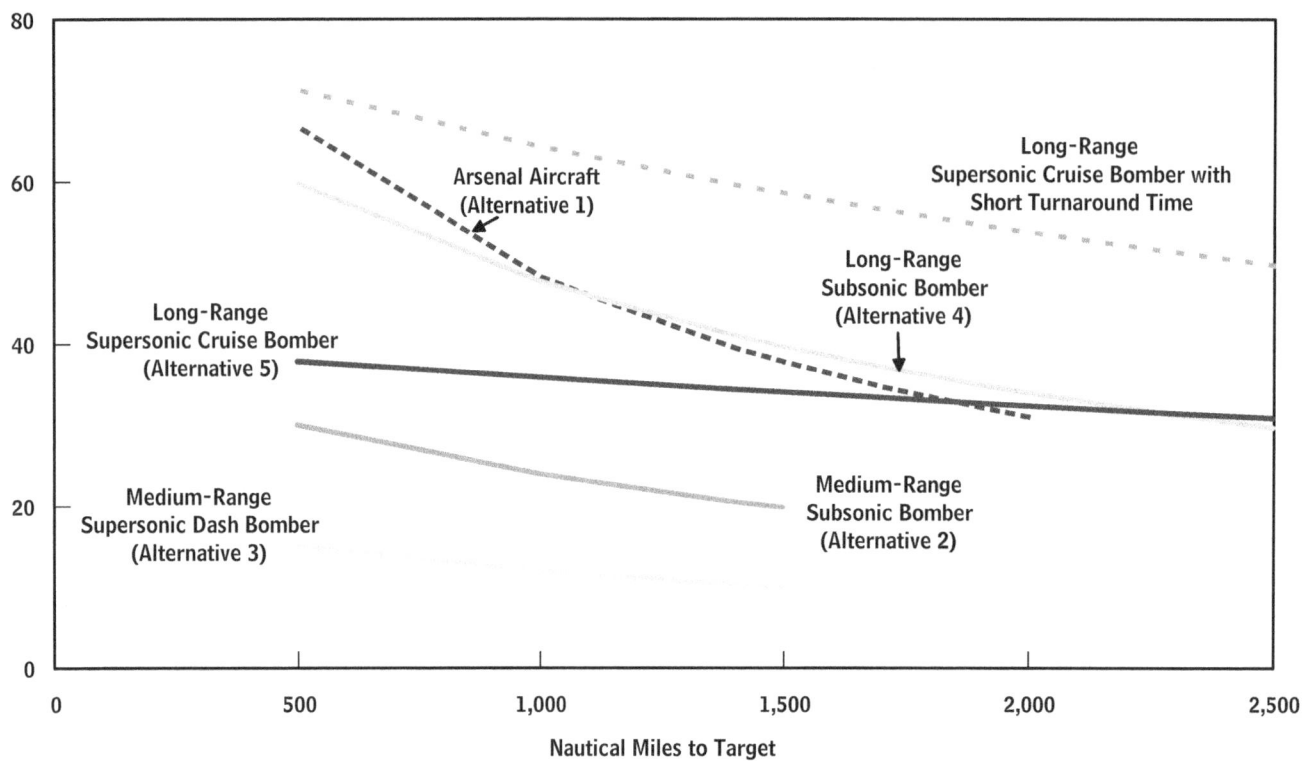

Source: Congressional Budget Office.

Notes: Data are shown out to the unrefueled radius of each type of aircraft when carrying a full bomb load. All alternatives could achieve greater ranges with aerial refueling or reduced bomb loads.

JDAM = Joint Direct Attack Munition.

but similar to one another's when measured in terms of equivalent warhead weight.[10] As a result, the relative performance of those alternatives depends on mission distance because speed and turn times are the differentiating factors. At short ranges, the arsenal aircraft (Alternative 1) and the long-range subsonic bomber (Alternative 4) offer the highest bomb delivery rates because they have shorter turn times than those of the long-range supersonic cruise bomber (Alternative 5). The arsenal aircraft is the highest at the shortest ranges because a substantial portion of the mission is flown by the missile at Mach 3. At ranges above about 1,000 nm, the higher payload and aircraft

speed allow the long-range subsonic bomber to overtake the arsenal aircraft. The long-range supersonic cruise bomber has a lower bomb delivery rate than that of the other two large-payload aircraft because CBO assumed a significantly longer turn time (about double) for that more advanced aircraft. Longer turn times would be likely because Alternative 5 would have four highly advanced engines versus two engines that would be derivatives of proven designs and because the greater rigors of sustained supersonic flight would require more careful servicing of the aircraft during its time on the ground. The higher speed of the bomber in Alternative 5 does result in shorter missions, however, allowing that alternative to overcome the disadvantage of longer ground times for longer-range missions. If the turn time for Alternative 5 were the same as for Alternatives 1 and 4, its delivery rate would be the highest at all mission distances— slightly higher than the arsenal aircraft at 500 nm, with a

---

10. With Alternative 1, the supersonic missile, the total payload weight of the C-17 is much higher than that of the long-range-bomber alternative, but most of that weight is associated with the launch racks, missile canisters, and the missile motor, not with the warheads.

Table 3-2.

Examples of Target Types for Air-to-Ground Missions

Type	Examples	Preferred Weapons
Hard Point	Deeply buried bunker	Unitary penetrators
	Hardened aircraft shelter	
Hard Area	Dispersed armored vehicles	Penetrating submunitions with target seekers
		Guided shaped charge weapons
Soft Point	Buildings	Unitary blast/ fragmentation
Soft Area	Supply dumps	Unitary blast/ fragmentation
	Dispersed trucks	Bomblet submunitions

Source: Congressional Budget Office.

Note: The terms "hard" and "soft" characterize the extent to which a target is vulnerable to a weapon's effects such as its blast wave or its metal fragmentation pattern. The terms "point" and "area" characterize the spatial extent of a target.

growing advantage as mission distance increased. (That case is shown as the dashed line in Figure 3-6.)

Payload Flexibility

Payload flexibility is a strike system's ability to deliver munitions with the most appropriate warhead for a given mission. The desired warhead is usually dictated by target characteristics. In particular, a target's "hardness" (its level of armor or other protection) and size (how easy it is to hit) combine to influence the choice of warhead. At the highest level, targets are grouped in four ways that match up against four types of warhead (see Table 3-2). The target types shown in the table represent generally preferred target/weapon combinations. In many cases, a warhead other than the preferred one could suffice. For example, unitary blast/fragmentation warheads can be effective against trucks if the trucks are arrayed close enough together. In other cases, only one type of warhead would be effective. For example, only ground-penetrating weapons could destroy hardened, deeply buried targets. (Other warhead types might be able to damage such facilities by

attacking exposed features such as doors or ventilation entrances.)

The penetrating-aircraft alternatives (2 through 5) would offer the greatest payload flexibility among CBO's long-range strike alternatives because they could be designed to carry all (or nearly all) existing or planned air-delivered munitions. Different types of warheads could be developed for the supersonic air-launched missile and the CAVs, but they would not be easily interchangeable and would require assumptions about what distribution of warhead types would be needed in the future. After being launched into orbit, the space-based CAV warheads could not be changed. The development of different versions of each missile would also increase the costs of the alternatives. CBO's cost estimates assume that the CAVs and the supersonic air-launched missile would be armed with simple unitary warheads. More complicated warheads—such as submunitions that require dispensing mechanisms or warheads with seekers for greater accuracy—would be more costly to develop and integrate into the missile systems.

Survivability

Survivability, the ability to complete a mission in the face of enemy air defenses and—except in the case of expendable systems such as the CAVs—return safely, is an important attribute for long-range strike systems because they would most likely be employed on missions lacking substantial air-defense suppression support. Those types of missions might include short-notice precision strikes that must be executed before enemy air defenses can be suppressed or missions conducted early in regional conflicts when suppression support might be available but when a potentially dangerous air-defense threat could still remain. As with responsiveness and firepower, substantially different survivability characteristics exist for CBO's long-range strike alternatives—differences that would influence the circumstances under which they could be employed.

The CAV alternatives would have the highest survivability against current air-defense systems and any new systems that might be expected in the near future. After a CAV is launched, its combination of hypersonic speed, small size, and maneuverability—which means it does not travel a predictable ballistic trajectory—makes it a difficult target that only sophisticated ballistic missile defenses, which do not exist today, could defeat. A CAV would be a challenging target even in cases requiring it to expend much of its speed to reach targets at the limits of its crossrange capability. Directed energy weapons, such as lasers, might eventually be able to defeat a CAV, although such technologies are in their infancy, and the CAV's thermal shielding against atmospheric heating would make it inherently resistant to such defensive measures.

Attacking a CAV system before it launches a missile would also be difficult. The surface-based CAVs would be located in secure areas far from an adversary's country—in the United States for the long-range CAV and perhaps at sea for the medium-range CAV. Consequently, attack from the ground would be difficult, and an adversary would need a long-range strike system to attack by air. Attacking the orbiting CAVs would require an advanced antisatellite system capable of hitting a target in equatorial low-Earth orbit. Although there is concern in DoD about the vulnerability of space systems in the future, the existence of antisatellite systems, other than those explored by the United States and the Soviet Union during the Cold War, has not been confirmed.[11]

The survivability of the arsenal aircraft would be limited by the C-17 launch platform. The missile itself would be difficult for air defenses to engage because of its high speed, small size, and its potential to be designed to incorporate some stealth characteristics. However, the system's survivability would be high only if the C-17 could remain beyond the reach of enemy air defenses. The C-17 is not stealthy and could be detected and tracked by radar. Modern surface-to-air missile (SAM) systems, if located on a country's border, could force the C-17 to remain well outside the enemy's border, seriously limiting the effective reach of the 500-nm supersonic missile. For example, the Russian-built SA-20 system is reported to have a maximum range of slightly over 100 nm.[12] Enemy fighters could also be a serious threat because they could

choose to cross their borders and intercept the C-17s even farther out. That threat could only be countered by U.S. fighter support if air-superiority fighters were already present in the region.

The survivability picture is more complicated for the alternatives that use penetrating stealthy bombers. The very low observable characteristics of the medium-range bombers and the long-range subsonic bomber (Alternatives 2 through 4) would offer good survivability against surface air defenses for operations in darkness and probably also in daylight, although advanced optical systems might be able to detect a high-altitude aircraft in daylight and cue a SAM intercept. Enemy interceptors at altitudes similar to those of the bombers could be a serious daytime threat, however. They could more easily detect the bombers, either visually by their crews or with long-range cameras, and such detection could occur at ranges short enough for air-to-air missiles or cannons to be effective. To help counter that threat, the bombers could be armed with air-to-air missiles of their own, but their slower speed and lack of maneuverability relative to fighters would still put them at a disadvantage. Alternative 3 could have good survivability against that threat because the bomber could turn away and try to escape at supersonic speed. Although interceptors might be faster, if the bomber began its escape early enough, its greater endurance could allow it to remain out of range long enough for the interceptors to exhaust their fuel. The fighters would not have destroyed the bomber, but they would have prevented it from completing its mission. As with the arsenal aircraft, the air-to-air threat would be lower if friendly fighters were available to support the bombers.

Although less stealthy than the other penetrating bombers, the long-range supersonic cruise bomber (Alternative 5) would have the advantage of even higher speed. That speed would shrink the effective range of SAM systems by reducing the amount of time available for an engagement. Although the bomber might be detected at a greater distance, it could pass beyond the range of the SAM before it was overtaken by the missile. Similarly, the ability to sustain a speed of Mach 2.4 would make it difficult for airborne interceptors to catch the bomber. That could give the aircraft in Alternative 5 better daytime survivability than the slower aircraft alternatives would have.

---

11. The antisatellite mission against a CAV is made more difficult because, except for countries on the equator, the CAV satellite does not pass directly over its target. Consequently, more powerful booster rockets would be needed to reach a CAV orbit, and a ground-based antisatellite laser would, in most cases, not have a direct line of sight to the satellites.

12. Duncan Lennox, ed., *Jane's Strategic Weapons Systems,* Issue 43 (July 2005).

Cost and Force-Structure Implications

The long-range strike alternatives the Congressional Budget Office examined would offer diverse capabilities. No single alternative provides superior effectiveness across all of the focus areas for long-range strike capability. In addition to simple differences in capability, each alternative would fit into the existing force structure in different ways. For example, fielding common aero vehicles would provide a new rapid-strike capability but could not replace the firepower offered by today's bombers when those aircraft are retired from service. A supersonic bomber, on the other hand, could replace the aged bombers but would offer significantly less improvement in responsiveness than CAVs would. Because of such distinctions, the alternatives CBO examined should not necessarily be viewed as mutually exclusive. Depending on how the Department of Defense eventually defines its requirements for long-range strike capability, a mix of different systems might be needed.

Further complicating comparison of the alternatives are the significant differences in the estimated costs to develop and field them (see Table 4-1). Research, development, test, and evaluation (RDT&E) costs could vary by over an order of magnitude, CBO estimates, with the missile alternatives at the lower end and the advanced supersonic bomber at the upper end. CBO's estimates of production costs vary over a similarly broad range, although the variation results in part from assumptions about how many of each type of system would be procured. In the absence of established DoD requirements, CBO chose quantities consistent with current force-structure plans and the procurement of past systems. Details of the methods CBO used to develop its cost estimates (with the exception of assumed procurement quantities) are described in the appendix. This chapter describes the assumptions underlying the procurement quantities used in the cost estimates and discusses the effect that cost and force-structure considerations, in conjunction with the capabilities described in Chapter 3,

could have on decisions about which future long-range strike systems might be pursued.

Aircraft-Based Systems—Alternatives 1 Through 5

The alternatives that include new aircraft designs would be significantly more costly to develop and procure than the alternatives that only develop new missiles, CBO estimates.[1] Aircraft development costs tend to be higher than missile development costs because of an aircraft's much greater complexity and size, as well as having to be designed for many years of operation rather than a single, one-way mission. Consequently, it is unlikely that DoD would simultaneously pursue more than one alternative for long-range aircraft. However, combinations of aircraft-based and missile-based alternatives could provide capabilities that DoD might judge to be cost-effective.

Alternative 1: Arsenal Aircraft with Supersonic Missiles

Along with the surface-based CAVs, the arsenal-aircraft alternative, at just over $4 billion, would be among the least expensive of the alternatives CBO examined if DoD chose to not purchase additional C-17s as dedicated launch platforms. DoD has nearly completed purchasing 180 C-17s for strategic and tactical airlift missions, and some of those aircraft could be used to deliver missiles. The 2,000 missiles slated for purchase under Alternative 1 would be a quantity on a par with the number in other tactical missile systems such as the Navy's Joint Standoff

---

1. The difference between the aircraft-based and missile-based alternatives would be even greater if operation and support costs were included. CBO focused on acquisition costs for those comparisons because they are sufficient for assessing top-level distinctions among the various alternatives.

Table 4-1.

Estimated Costs of Long-Range Strike Alternatives Examined by CBO

		Costs[a] (Billions of 2006 dollars)			Average Unit Procurement Cost (Millions of 2006 dollars)
	Quantity	RDT&E	Procurement	Total[b]	
1 Arsenal Aircraft	2,000 [c]	1.5	2.8/6.1 [c]	4.3/7.6 [c]	1.4 [d]
2 Medium-Range Subsonic Bomber	275	19	52	72	188
3 Medium-Range Supersonic Dash Bomber	275	23	61	85	220
4 Long-Range Subsonic Bomber	150	31	61	93	409
5 Long-Range Supersonic Cruise Bomber	150	69	137	207	912
6 Medium-Range Surface-Based CAV	48	2.4	1.2	3.7	26
7 Long-Range Surface-Based CAV[e]	24	2.5	0.9	4.0	36
8 Space-Based CAV	128 [f]	4.0	7.7	11.7	55

Source: Congressional Budget Office.

Note: RDT&E = research, development, test, and evaluation; CAV = common aero vehicle.

a.   The costs for Alternatives 2 to 5 exclude munitions.

b.   Includes additional military construction costs of about $1 billion for the aircraft alternatives (2 to 5) and $600 million for Alternative 7.

c.   The quantity shown is the number of supersonic missiles purchased. The lower of the two costs assumes that those missiles would be carried by C-17 aircraft in the current fleet. The higher of the two costs assumes that 15 additional C-17s would be purchased to support the strike mission.

d.   Average unit procurement cost is for supersonic missiles only.

e.   Alternative 7 assumes that 24 Peacekeeper missiles would be converted to carry two CAVs per missile. If more missiles were desired, as many as 60 Peacekeepers might be available for conversion. The cost of additional missiles would be much higher than the cost shown here because new boosters would be needed.

f.   Enough satellites would be purchased to maintain the constellation for 30 years. Only 40 space-based CAVs would be available for use at any one time.

Weapon (JSOW) and the Air Force's Joint Air-to-Surface Standoff Missile (JASSM).

If DoD decided that aircraft dedicated to the strike mission were needed, procuring 15 additional C-17 aircraft would cost about $3.3 billion, CBO estimates. That number of aircraft could maintain continuous coverage of about 45,000 square nautical miles with a 10-minute response time. The estimated cost for those additional aircraft would be considerably higher, however, if the decision to purchase them was not made before the C-17 production line closed. Because the 2006 Quadrennial Defense Review did not identify plans to purchase more

than 180 C-17s, currently planned production will end by 2010. Purchasing additional aircraft would have the advantage of being able to augment the airlift fleet when they are not needed as strike aircraft. Alternatively, C-17s from the air-mobility fleet could be pressed into service as strikers if the circumstances required, although that would decrease the number of C-17s available to move cargo.

In many respects, the arsenal aircraft would offer performance similar to that of the long-range subsonic penetrating bomber (Alternative 4), albeit for shorter distances. For example, the two alternatives would have similar firepower up to about 2,000 nautical miles and would require a similar number of aircraft to maintain responsive strike orbits up to 1,500 nm from a base or aerial refueling point. A major disadvantage of Alternative 1, however, would be the aircraft's lack of stealth, which would make it unable to enter hostile airspace until after defenses had been suppressed. For strike missions without defense suppression support, Alternative 1 would have a penetration depth equal to only its missile's range, about 500 nm—a distance only on the order of that for short-range fighters. Penetration of hostile airspace would be further limited if enemy fighters were able to fly out beyond their borders to intercept the C-17s. Increasing the range of the missile could alleviate that shortcoming but at higher cost and a smaller carriage capability on the aircraft.

To overcome the disadvantages of delivery from a non-stealthy C-17, Alternative 1's missile could be developed in conjunction with a stealthy bomber. The size and weight of the notional missile are similar to those of GBU-28 bunker-buster bombs that can be delivered by B-2 bombers. Any of the aircraft alternatives could be designed to accommodate the supersonic missile, although it would be most difficult to fit such bulky weapons into the smaller medium-range supersonic dash bomber in Alternative 3. If a long-range bomber (or one of today's B-2s) was to carry it, the supersonic missile would enjoy the advantages of stealth, global delivery range, and rapid responsiveness (from an orbiting aircraft) against fleeting targets. Integrating the missile onto more than one aircraft would require additional development costs because the missile would probably be launched in different ways: from a container in an arsenal aircraft, from a rotary launcher in a penetrating bomber's internal weapons bay, or from an external weapons station on an F-15E. Responsiveness at global ranges would still lag far behind that of the CAV alternatives, however.

Alternatives 2 and 3: Medium-Range Bombers

The medium-range stealth bombers would improve strike capabilities over regional distances but would not be as well suited for missions with a global range, although such missions might be possible with extensive tanker support. As a result, medium-range bombers would probably not be a suitable replacement for some of the capabilities offered by today's long-range heavy bombers. CBO assumed instead that DoD would purchase about 275 of the aircraft as replacements for F-117 stealth fighters and F-15E Strike Eagles.[2] For that number of aircraft,

a medium-range subsonic bomber force (Alternative 2) would cost about $72 billion, and a medium-range supersonic dash bomber force (Alternative 3) would cost about $85 billion, CBO estimates. The result would be to provide substantial firepower capability at ranges beyond those of today's strike fighters but no improvement at heavy-bomber ranges (see Figure 4-1). That result is illustrated by the additional delivery capability beyond 700 nm—about a 70 percent increase for Alternative 2 and about a 35 percent increase for Alternative 3 for ranges up to 1,500 nm. For ranges greater than 1,500 nm, the improvement offered by the medium-range bombers drops quickly because the aircraft must carry reduced bomb loads to fly those distances. In addition to having greater range, that entire portion of the force would be stealthy. Today, there are only 55 stealthy F-117s that are operational compared with 217 conventional F-15Es. Depending on the alternative selected, however, the new force could lack the air-to-air capability of the dual-role F-15E.

The purchase of 275 aircraft under Alternatives 2 and 3 would increase delivery capability at short ranges relative to that of today's force but by a smaller proportion (as shown in Figure 4-1). As an alternative, those notional forces could be sized to match today's short-range capability, although that would result in a lesser improvement between 900 nm and 1,500 nm—about 22 percent. Such a force would need either 85 medium-range subsonic bombers or 170 medium-range supersonic dash bombers. For those purchase quantities, the costs of Alternatives 2 and 3 would drop to about $42 billion and $66 billion, respectively, CBO estimates.

Although medium-range bombers alone could not replace all of the capabilities of heavy bombers, a medium-range bomber force in concert with one of the CAV alternatives would provide a capability that some might argue could reduce or eliminate the need for heavy bombers. The CAVs would provide prompt strike at global ranges, and the medium-range bombers would provide substantial firepower for regional conflicts. Replacing heavy

---

2. This approach assumes that the fraction of the inventory that is maintained in a combat-ready status is similar for both the current aircraft and the aircraft in CBO's alternatives. Although surface CAV missiles would require periodic maintenance, their combat-ready status could be nearly 100 percent. The space-based CAVs would have a 100 percent combat-capable rate unless there were irreparable failures while in orbit.

Figure 4-1.

Potential Firepower of Alternative Air Force Strike Forces, Without Aerial Refueling

(Number of 2,000-pound JDAM-equivalents per day)

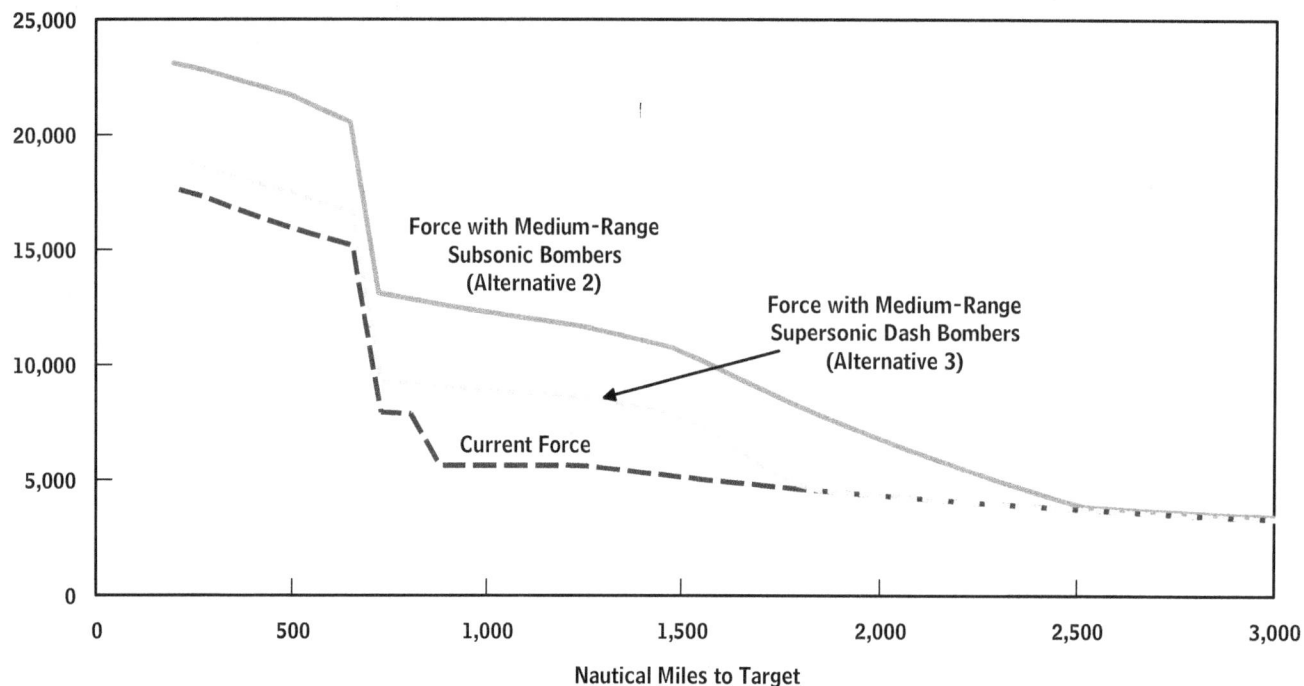

Source: Congressional Budget Office.

Notes: Future forces are assumed to retain current bombers and short-range fighters but to replace today's F-15Es and F-117As with 275 medium-range subsonic or supersonic bombers.

This figure is based on the Air Force's total inventory of aircraft. Numbers for combat-ready aircraft would be lower.

JDAM = Joint Direct Attack Munition.

bombers with CAVs for global missions would have the disadvantage of reducing firepower over global ranges. Although missions of long durations over global ranges limit the sortie rates of today's bombers to well below one mission per aircraft per day, large long-range bomber forces could still deliver a considerable number of bombs per day.[3] For example, a B-2 with a payload of 16 Joint Direct Attack Munitions could generate an average delivery rate of about three to four JDAM per aircraft per day. When multiplied by many bombers in a large force, that delivery rate would exceed one that would be practical with long-range CAVs. Historically, however, global-range conventional strikes such as the B-2 missions from Missouri to Bosnia have involved only small numbers of

bombers. That may be because target sets have been small or because only stealth aircraft—and hence only a small fraction of the bomber force—were suitable for those missions.

Alternative 3 is similar to Alternative 2 in terms of range and cruise speed. The additional ability to dash at Mach 1.5 comes with the penalty of having half the payload of the medium-range subsonic bomber and an estimated cost about 20 percent higher—$85 billion versus $72 billion—for the same production quantity of 275 aircraft. As with Alternative 2, this alternative would provide significantly improved strike capability relative to the F-117 and F-15E fighters that would be replaced.

Alternative 3 would have a sizable advantage—about a factor of two for orbits less than 1,000 nm from the last refueling base or tanker—over Alternative 2 with respect

---

3.   Bombers are often deployed to forward locations during sustained operations to overcome the limitation of that sortie rate.

Figure 4-2.

Total Potential Firepower of Alternative Bomber Forces, by Mission Distance

(Number of 2,000-pound JDAM-equivalents per day)

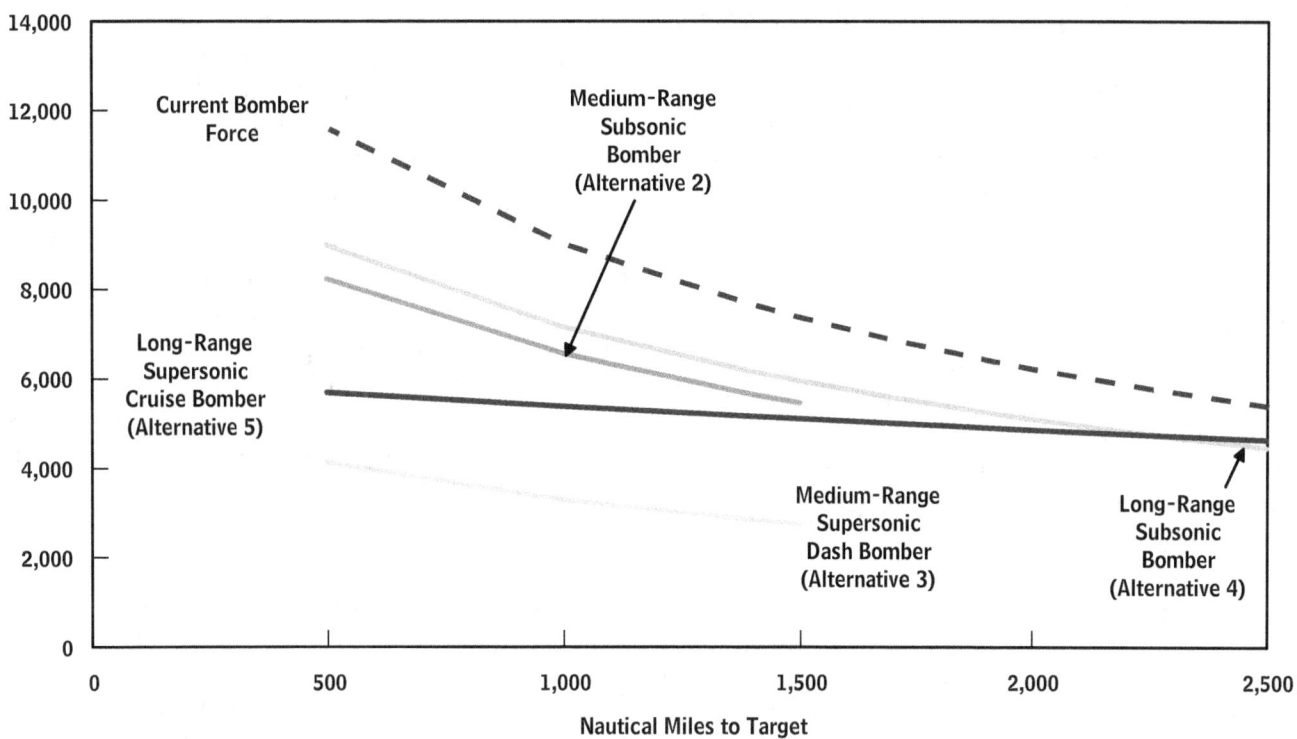

Nautical Miles to Target

Source: Congressional Budget Office.

Notes: Data are shown out to the unrefueled radius of each type of aircraft when carrying a full bomb load. All alternatives could achieve greater ranges with aerial refueling or reduced bomb loads.

This figure is based on the total number of aircraft purchased. Numbers for combat-ready aircraft would be lower.

The arsenal aircraft (Alternative 1) is not shown because that alternative does not assume a specific quantity of aircraft.

Unlike the display in Figure 4-1, the current bomber force firepower is shown here without daily sortie constraints.

to the number of aircraft needed to maintain very short response times against time-critical targets because the bomber's supersonic dash speed would allow it to attack targets at greater distances within a given response time. However, the lower payload for Alternative 3 could negate that advantage somewhat if the aircraft had to attack targets at a rate that would exhaust its munitions well before its fuel. The lower payload would result in significantly lower firepower than that of the subsonic bomber, which could deliver munitions at about twice the rate of the supersonic dash bomber during sustained operations.

Proponents of an aircraft similar to the supersonic bomber in Alternative 3 argue that its superior ability to elude enemy fighter aircraft could be an important advantage, especially for daytime strike missions. As was

discussed in Chapter 3, however, those circumstances might be rather narrow, and, if the bomber was confronted by enemy fighters on the way to the target, the act of eluding the fighters might prevent it from completing its mission.

Alternatives 4 and 5: Long-Range Bombers

Long-range stealth bombers would improve strike capabilities over global distances. The subsonic bomber (Alternative 4) would require tanker support comparable with that of today's bombers. The supersonic cruise bomber (Alternative 5) would require greater tanker support because of its high fuel consumption. CBO assumed that DoD would purchase about 150 of the aircraft as replacements for the B-1, B-2, and B-52. Despite the similarity in numbers to the current bomber force, that replacement would result in some changes in firepower capability (see Figure 4-2). For the long-range subsonic bomber in Alternative 4, a smaller inventory (150 under CBO's notional alternative versus 182 bombers currently in place) plus a lower payload relative to that of the B-1 and B-52 would result in less total delivery capability than that of the current force. In practice, the difference might be smaller than shown in the figure if the Air Force could maintain a larger fraction of the new bombers in combat-ready status. The actual number of new bombers DoD might decide it needs would depend on that consideration as well as assessments of future requirements.

The lower inventory and lower payload of the long-range supersonic cruise bomber in Alternative 5 relative to those of the B-1 and B-52 would also result in lower firepower at shorter ranges, but the faster bomber's shorter mission time would reduce that difference for longer mission distances. As with the medium-range-bomber alternatives, Alternatives 4 and 5 would result in an all-stealth bomber force.[4] Today, there are only 21 stealthy B-2s compared with 161 conventional B-1s and B-52s.

CBO's estimate of Alternative 4's cost—$93 billion—is somewhat higher than the cost for the medium-range-bomber alternatives—$72 billion for Alternative 2 and $85 billion for Alternative 3—but only about half the number of aircraft would be purchased. Despite its lower numbers, Alternative 4 would still outperform the alternatives for medium-range bombers in terms of firepower. However, only 25 additional medium-range subsonic bombers—for a total of 300—would be needed for Alternative 2 to match the firepower of Alternative 4 at ranges up to 1,500 nm. CBO estimates that adding those aircraft would increase the cost of Alternative 2 to about $74 billion, a total lower than the total cost for 150 long-range subsonic bombers. In contrast, because of the lower payload of the medium-range supersonic dash bombers in Alternative 3, about 600 of those would be needed to match the firepower of the long-range subsonic bomber in Alternative 4. That large force would cost about $131 billion, CBO estimates.

The long-range supersonic cruise bomber in Alternative 5 is the most advanced concept examined in this study.

Whereas the other aircraft could use many technologies already developed for existing systems, Alternative 5 would represent an all-new design. Consequently, it would come with a much higher price tag—about $207 billion to develop and field 150 bombers, CBO estimates. That is more than double the estimated costs for Alternatives 3 and 4 and nearly triple the cost of Alternative 2. For its higher price, the long-range supersonic cruise bomber would offer capabilities between those of subsonic bombers and CAVs. At short mission distances, the supersonic bomber in Alternative 5 would offer modest improvements in responsiveness relative to subsonic aircraft but with lower sustained munitions delivery rates (firepower). At very long ranges, Alternative 5 would offer the greatest firepower but would be far less responsive than would the CAV alternatives. Depending on the level of stealth that could be incorporated into its high-speed design, the bomber in Alternative 5 might have better survivability than that of the other aircraft alternatives because its high speed would give both air and ground threats little time to engage it. However, CAVs would have a better chance of reaching their targets.

The performance and cost of the bomber in Alternative 5 suggest it would be a preferred system only under a narrow set of requirements—specifically, if large rates of munitions delivery are desired over global distances where the bomber's speed and range combine to give it a substantial firepower advantage over the other alternatives. Such situations, however, would probably occur rarely or not at all. The rapid delivery of large numbers of munitions is typically associated with conflicts that include substantial forces on the ground, which implicitly suggests that some regional access for strike aircraft would be available. Aircraft carriers could provide strike capability far from the United States against those targets that can be reached from the sea until regional bases could be established. Time-sensitive targets, those for which there is not time to move a carrier into position or to fly to from the United States at subsonic speed, typically do not require a great volume of firepower but rather a few well-placed bombs. In those cases, the CAV alternatives could offer adequate firepower and much better responsiveness than the bomber in Alternative 5. Consequently, it could be argued that an approach that develops a CAV option and a new subsonic bomber would provide more broadly useful capabilities at less cost than would a long-range supersonic cruise bomber.

---

4.   As was noted in Chapter 3, the supersonic cruise bomber would be less stealthy than the other alternatives because it would rely only on its shape to achieve its low-observable characteristics. Its very high speed, however, would augment its survivability.

Common Aero Vehicle Systems— Alternatives 6 Through 8

The common aero vehicle alternatives would offer much shorter response times than those of the aircraft-based alternatives for missions over long distances because of their hypersonic speeds. For missions where the launch platform can loiter close to target areas, the CAVs do not perform as well because their launchers must be located at a considerable distance from enemy territory—at a secure base or on a ship in the region for the medium-range CAV (Alternative 6), in the United States for the long-range CAV (Alternative 7), and several hundred miles away in low-Earth orbit for the space-based CAV (Alternative 8). The CAV alternatives would be much less expensive than developing new penetrating bombers, CBO estimates, but somewhat more expensive than the air-launched missile in the arsenal-aircraft alternative (for the quantities considered). As was mentioned earlier, the quantity purchased under each CAV alternative was set to give the alternatives as similar a capability as possible. A constellation of five satellites in equatorial low-Earth orbit would provide the space-based CAV with a response time at least as good as that of the long-range surface CAV. In CBO's alternative, arming each launcher with eight CAVs provided a launch mass well suited to available space-launch rockets. The resulting quantity totaled 40 operational CAVs in orbit. However, satellites in low-Earth orbit typically have about a 10-year life in the harsh environment of space. Consequently, CBO assumed that two additional constellations' worth of satellites would be needed to maintain that capability over about 30 years, a service life similar to what is often expected for new military aircraft. The surface-based alternatives had the same number of test and operational missiles as a single space-based constellation did to provide similar total firepower.[5] Additional CAVs could be purchased under any of the alternatives, although the unit cost for the missiles under Alternative 7 would increase dramatically when the inventory of retired Peacekeeper missiles was exhausted and new intercontinental ballistic missile-sized rockets had to be purchased as well. A new rocket the size of a Peacekeeper would cost about $100 million and require new development, CBO estimates, more than tripling the

cost of the round. Alternatively, it might be possible to purchase submarine-launched Trident D-5 boosters that are currently in production at about $40 million each and convert them for surface launch.[6] The CAV missiles are much more expensive on a per-round basis than are Alternative 1's air-launched missiles, but they would provide much higher speed and much harder hitting power. Because each medium-range CAV would have a lower unit cost, total costs associated with a medium-range CAV force would increase more slowly as purchase quantity increased.

High unit costs would probably make CAVs unsuitable for replacing aircraft in roles that require attacking large numbers of targets. For example, with aerial refueling support, 100 long-range supersonic cruise bombers (Alternative 5)—the fraction of a 150-aircraft fleet that might be committed to a conflict—could deliver a payload equivalent to about 2,100 JDAMs per day to a range of 7,000 nm.[7] The procurement cost for a similar number of space-based CAVs would total over $200 billion (see Figure 4-3). The costs for that number of weapons would be about $30 billion for the medium-range surface CAV and $80 billion for the long-range surface-launched CAV.[8] The aircraft alternatives' costs change little with increasing numbers of weapons delivered because the costs of those weapons are small compared with the costs of the aircraft. (Alternative 1 has the lowest cost, but as noted earlier, it is considerably less capable than the other alternatives.) Aside from the cost involved in achieving high delivery rates with CAVs, other practical difficulties exist. For example, forward deployment of several hundred medium-range CAVs would be a significant transportation burden, and substantial additional launch facilities would be needed to provide high rates of fire with

---

5. Alternative 7 included half as many missiles, but each missile could deliver two CAVs. Although that arrangement would be less flexible than a one CAV/one missile configuration, a target of high enough value to warrant a CAV shot might warrant two warheads to improve the odds that the target would be destroyed.

6. The 2006 Quadrennial Defense Review includes plans to rapidly develop a system that would deliver conventional warheads on Trident missiles. Those missiles would probably be launched from Trident submarines instead of converted for launch from the ground or from surface ships.

7. CBO used 100 aircraft, not the entire 150-aircraft force, to reflect aircraft that might not be mission-capable at any given time. That distinction was less important for aircraft-to-aircraft comparisons. CBO used entire inventories under the assumption that comparable fractions of each type would be operational.

8. The unit cost of the long-range surface-launched CAVs that require new production of boosters is more than double that of the medium-range version but provides two CAVs per shot.

Figure 4-3.

Cumulative Development and Acquisition Costs for Weapons and Their Delivery Systems, by Number of Weapons Used

(Billions of 2006 dollars)

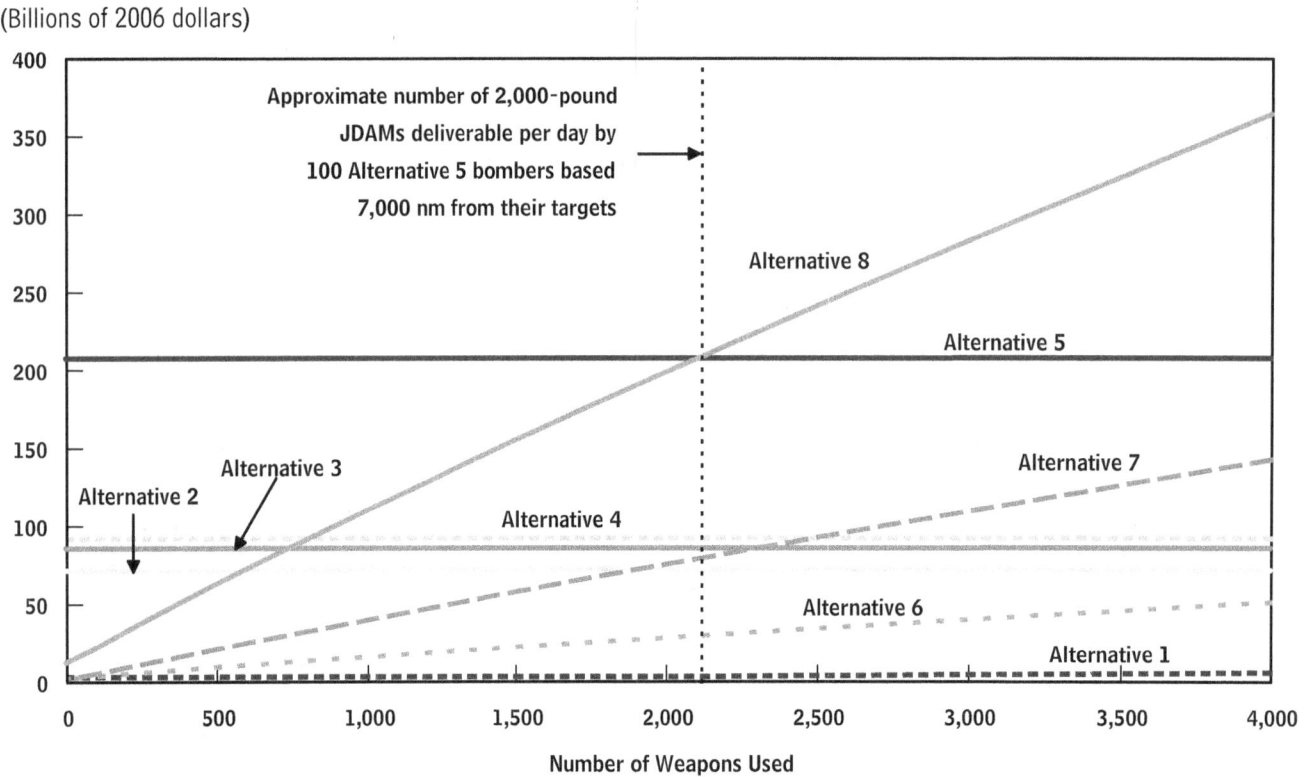

Source: Congressional Budget Office.

Notes: Assumes aircraft are delivering 2,000-pound Joint Direct Attack Munitions (JDAMs).

nm = nautical miles.

Alternative 1 = Arsenal aircraft
Alternative 2 = Medium-range subsonic bomber
Alternative 3 = Medium-range supersonic dash bomber
Alternative 4 = Long-range subsonic bomber
Alternative 5 = Long-range supersonic cruise bomber
Alternative 6 = Medium-range surface-based common aero vehicle
Alternative 7 = Long-range surface-based common aero vehicle
Alternative 8 = Space-based common aero vehicle

long-range surface CAVs. Similarly, large numbers of space-based CAVs would require a proportionally larger number of Evolved Expendable Launch Vehicles to put them in orbit and hence might require an expansion of the nation's space-launch infrastructure. Consequently, CAVs most likely would be cost-effective only against high-value targets that typically exist in small numbers. However, as was discussed earlier, a combination of long-range CAVs and medium-range bombers could conceivably replace long-range bombers if DoD decided that sufficient CAVs could be purchased to handle the number of targets that would require attack from global distances.

It might also prove cost-effective to purchase a combination of the missiles in Alternatives 6 and 7. Much of the research and development cost, particularly that of the reentry vehicle, could be the same for the two systems. The medium-range CAVs, which could be purchased in larger quantities for a given level of investment, could be stationed at forward locations such as Guam or on ships so as to be in a position to provide short response times in areas of heightened tension, and the longer-range missiles could be saved for circumstances when the medium-range systems were not located close enough to targets that might arise.

The Relative Difficulty of Developing the Long-Range Strike Alternatives Considered by CBO

The force-structure comparisons described above are in the context of fully operational forces that might eventually be fielded. Those comparisons do not consider the different lengths of time for development and procurement that might be needed to realize such forces, a factor that could be important as threats evolve and as existing systems age and are retired. The time required to develop a weapon system is influenced by many factors, some of which are inherent to the system (for example, the maturity of component technologies) and others that are external to the system (for example, funding levels and institutional support). This section briefly discusses how factors that are inherent to developing new systems could influence how soon the alternatives examined by CBO might be fielded.

Determining a schedule on which the development of a long-range strike alternative might proceed requires detailed information regarding the work and testing to be accomplished. CBO lacks that information for the alternatives considered in this study, and even if such information were available, DoD's experience indicates that predicting schedules for any of its major programs before they are well under way is problematic. Although CBO cannot provide definitive schedules for developing long-range strike alternatives, it can provide observations indicating the relative difficulty of implementing those alternatives.

The United States does not currently have an operational supersonic cruise missile, but other nations, such as Russia and India, do. The supersonic missiles that currently exist, however, lack the range and payload postulated for the missile used in the arsenal-aircraft alternative considered by CBO. Nonetheless, the United States has investigated the technologies needed for such a missile for a number of years. For example, in April 2002, the Defense Threat Reduction Agency solicited information on technology available for executing an advanced concept technology demonstration program for a supersonic cruise missile. Because supersonic cruise missiles exist and the technology needed to build them is relatively well understood, the arsenal aircraft (Alternative 1) would probably require less time to develop than the other alternatives for long-range strike considered by CBO.

Although the United States has test-flown maneuvering reentry vehicles, it must still develop the technology to field an operational CAV. In particular, materials would have to be developed that could withstand for up to 30 minutes the heat generated by the CAV's hypersonic flight through the atmosphere as it maneuvered to strike its intended target. In addition, although components of existing boosters might be used for the medium-range surface-based CAV, the integration of those components could prove problematic, as has been the case in an ongoing program to develop and deploy ballistic missile defenses. And the protective satellite that would house the space-based CAVs would have to be designed and tested. Therefore, the time and effort needed to develop either surface-based or space-based CAVs (Alternatives 6, 7, and 8) would most likely be greater than that to develop a supersonic cruise missile delivered by an arsenal aircraft.

The medium-range bombers (subsonic and with supersonic dash, Alternatives 2 and 3) and long-range subsonic bomber (Alternative 4) would all be based largely on existing technology, much of which has already been implemented in operational aircraft. Nonetheless, their development would require new aircraft designs (not merely modifications to existing designs), as well as the integration of a large number of subsystems, including complex software supporting the aircraft's flight and operation of its sensor systems. Therefore, those alternatives would probably take longer to develop than would the supersonic cruise missile or the common aero vehicle.

Of all the alternatives considered by CBO, the long-range supersonic cruise bomber (Alternative 5) would most likely require the greatest effort and time to develop. Although the United States has operated and test-flown supersonic bombers and reconnaissance aircraft in the past, many years have passed since a U.S. manufacturer designed such an aircraft in detail. Moreover, incorporating some amount of stealth (or radar cross-section reduction) in a supersonic cruise bomber would probably require the use of advanced materials not incorporated in past designs. As with the subsonic bombers, developing a supersonic bomber would require integrating a large number of subsystems and complex software. Achieving the engine fuel efficiencies postulated by CBO for this alternative would also require additional development of technology.

Appendix:
The Methodology Behind the Cost Analysis

The Congressional Budget Office (CBO) developed several alternatives for maintaining and improving the long-range strike capabilities of the U.S. military into the next decade. Those alternatives include upgrading tactical missile capabilities, improving the fleet of bomber aircraft, and building maneuverable reentry vehicles that are launched from ballistic missiles on the ground or from satellites in space.

For each alternative, CBO estimated the costs to develop and procure the weapon system, as well as the costs to improve or build the facilities and infrastructure needed to support the system.

Expenses in the development phase include the cost to design and build the components of the long-range strike system, the cost to test those components to ensure that they meet performance requirements, and the cost to integrate the system into the military's infrastructure and support systems. Expenses in the procurement phase include the cost of special tools and equipment to manufacture system components; the cost of hardware, material, and fabrication such as finished components and raw materials; and the cost to assemble the final product. Hardware, material, and fabrication are also important for determining estimates because they are inputs to statistical relationships used to estimate costs for nonrecurring design and other support costs.

All of the cost estimates in this appendix are presented in 2006 dollars. Significant uncertainty exists about the capabilities, technologies, and costs associated with developing, purchasing, and operating weapon systems envisioned in the alternatives. Because the programs are either conceptual in nature or in the early stages of development, they entail a greater risk of cost and schedule overruns than do programs that are better defined and based

on proven technologies. CBO's cost estimates represent one possible outcome, calculated under specific assumptions regarding technologies and capabilities. Although CBO attempted to account for that risk, those estimates will change, perhaps significantly, as the designs of the systems in the alternatives become more fully defined.

The Cost of Supersonic Cruise Missiles for the Arsenal Aircraft

In Alternative 1, the Air Force would develop and procure a new supersonic cruise missile that would be launched from an arsenal aircraft. Because the arsenal aircraft would be a modified version of an existing airframe (the C-17), for which the costs are generally known, this discussion focuses primarily on the methodology used to develop the cost of developing and procuring the missile.

The need to purchase additional C-17 aircraft would depend in large part on future airlift requirements. The projected fleet of 180 C-17 aircraft might be sufficient to perform the long-range strike mission without critically hampering concurrent airlift efforts; thus, there would be little additional costs beyond that of the missiles. However, if the existing fleet of aircraft was not sufficient to meet that new requirement, additional C-17s would need to be purchased. That could substantially increase the total cost of the arsenal aircraft alternative. On the basis of recent acquisition cost data from the ongoing procurement program, CBO estimated, for example, that acquiring 15 additional C-17s for that purpose would cost about $3.3 billion. That estimate assumes those aircraft would be purchased at the end of current planned production, before the assembly line was shut down. If the decision to purchase additional aircraft was delayed beyond 2008, that assembly line would have to be reestab-

Table A-1.

Characteristics of Supersonic Missiles for the Arsenal Aircraft (Alternative 1)

	Variable
Launch Weight (Pounds)	4,000
Maximum Speed	Mach 3
Payload	1,000-pound warhead
Range (Nautical miles)	500
Engine Design	Ramjet
Number of Engines	1

Source: Congressional Budget Office.

Note: Mach is the ratio of the speed of an object to the speed of sound in air.

lished. In that case, it would cost more to acquire additional aircraft.

Several variables for the performance parameters and design of a supersonic cruise missile drive the cost of such a weapon, although the exact values of those variables are not known at this time. For this study, CBO assumed that the missile would be capable of traveling 500 nautical miles and would carry a 1,000-pound warhead (see Table A-1 for a listing of the missile's characteristics).

The most important variable is the required speed of the weapon, which would affect the design—and thus the cost—of the propulsion system. The missile considered in this study would use a ramjet propulsion system with a top speed of Mach 3.[1, 2] The cost of a supersonic missile

is also affected by the type of warhead chosen for the system. CBO assumed that the missile would employ a less-expensive unitary warhead rather than precision submunitions that would require more advanced guidance and control systems to permit complex maneuvers by the missile in the moments before it reached its target. CBO estimated that the cost to develop and procure 2,000 such supersonic cruise missiles would total $4.3 billion, including the cost to integrate the weapon with a delivery aircraft such as the C-17 cargo plane. On average, it would cost $2.2 million to acquire those missiles (see Table A-2 for a summary of acquisition costs for this alternative).

CBO used several sources to estimate the development and procurement costs of a new supersonic cruise missile, such as methods and data contained in a 1998 cost estimate from the Naval Center for Cost Analysis for a ramjet missile, as well as information on hardware costs from existing ramjet/scramjet efforts.[3] CBO also looked at data from prior tactical missile programs and other cost studies (see Table A-3 for a summary of the methods used to estimate development and procurement costs for this alternative).

CBO's estimates for development and procurement are broken down into costs for:

■ Hardware, material, and fabrication;

■ Nonrecurring design, testing, and tooling; and

■ Other support such as program management, initial maintenance plans, and contractor fees.

Hardware, Material, and Fabrication

Hardware, material, and fabrication includes the cost of purchasing finished components and raw materials from subcontractors, as well as the cost of recurring labor associated with assembling the final product. Those costs are historically the most significant part of the cost estimate for missile production and also constitute a small portion of costs in the development phase. Hardware, material,

---

1. Mach is a ratio of the speed of an object to the speed of sound in the air or fluid in which it is traveling. At standard sea-level conditions, Mach 1 is 1,225 kilometers/hour (766 miles per hour) in the atmosphere.

2. In a typical turbojet engine, pressure is maintained in the combustion chamber through the use of a compressor fan. In contrast, a ramjet propulsion system uses the forward speed of the vehicle to "ram" external air into the combustion chamber to create the high pressure required for combustion. However, air entering a ramjet engine must be slowed down, as combustion can only take place at subsonic speeds, which limits a ramjet's top speed to about Mach 5. New supersonic combustion ramjet (scramjet) technology is attempting to overcome that limitation by allowing combustion to occur at supersonic speeds.

3. Jeff Cherwonik, William Stranges, and Jeff Wolfe, *Generic Supersonic Cruise Missile Life Cycle Cost Estimate,* prepared by the Naval Center for Cost Analysis in support of the Hard and Deeply Buried Target Defeat Capability Weapon Analysis of Alternatives (Arlington, Va.: Naval Center for Cost Analysis, October 1998).

Table A-2.

Acquisition Costs of Supersonic Missiles for the Arsenal Aircraft (Alternative 1)

(Billions of dollars)

	Cost
Research and Development	
Hardware, material, and fabrication[a]	0.1
Nonrecurring design, testing, and tooling[b]	0.8
Other support[c]	0.6
Subtotal, research and development	1.5
Procurement (2,000 missiles)	
Hardware, material, and fabrication	1.6
Nonrecurring design, testing, and tooling	0.2
Other support	1.0
Subtotal, procurement	2.8
Total Estimated Acquisition Costs	**4.3**

Source: Congressional Budget Office.

a. Includes the cost of purchasing finished components and raw materials from subcontractors and the cost of recurring labor associated with assembling the final product.

b. Includes one-time costs that do not vary with the total number of missiles produced. Those costs include initial design and engineering efforts, software development, systems testing and evaluation, flight-testing, and platform integration.

c. Includes costs for contractor and government program management, data collection, contractor fees, and initial maintenance agreements.

and fabrication are also important for cost-estimating purposes because they are inputs to statistical relationships CBO used to estimate costs for nonrecurring design and other support costs.

Tactical missiles typically contain four main hardware components: the engine, the airframe, the guidance and control system, and the warhead. In addition, CBO assumed that each missile would require a booster rocket to accelerate the weapon to a speed sufficient to operate the ramjet.[4] CBO estimated that hardware, material, and fabrication for the supersonic cruise missile would cost $140 million for the development phase and about $1.6 billion for the procurement phase.

CBO approximated the cost for the missile engine on the basis of the material and fabrication costs of propulsion

hardware in the X-43A hypersonic research aircraft, the GQM-163 missile (a supersonic sea-skimming target used to test shipboard defensive systems), and the Scramjet Engine Demonstration (SED) program.[5] The airframe cost estimate is based on the cost of other missile airframes, such as the Joint Standoff Weapon (JSOW), with adjustments for weight and material to account for the higher temperatures that a supersonic cruise missile would endure during flight.[6] The cost estimates for the guidance and control and warhead subsystems are based on analogies to other missile programs such as the Tomahawk cruise missile and the JSOW.

CBO assumed that the missile payload would consist of a unitary warhead, although it is possible that the Department of Defense (DoD) might add precision submunitions to a supersonic strike missile. However, such proposals would create additional technical challenges and costs that are not included in CBO's estimate. CBO used the cost of the Mk 72 booster from the Navy's Standard missile as an analogy to estimate the potential cost of the booster rocket because the Mk 72 propels a load that would be similar in weight to the proposed supersonic cruise missile. (CBO assumed that the missile and the booster considered in this alternative would weigh about 4,000 pounds.)

---

4. Ramjet engines use external air speed, generated by the velocity of the vehicle itself, to create the pressure in the engine necessary for combustion, but the air speed must first be provided by some other means before the ramjet engine can function. While there are several ways to generate that speed in a tactical missile system, CBO assumed this missile would use a solid rocket booster that would be jettisoned once the missile reached the necessary speed.

5. The costs can only be approximated because the programs mentioned above are not direct analogies to a missile propulsion system of the type that would be used in a new supersonic cruise missile. The scramjets used in the National Aeronautics and Space Administration's X-43A and the Air Force and the Defense Advanced Research Projects Agency's SED programs are only meant to be demonstration articles for use in testing and proving concepts. The GQM-163 is a missile used by the U.S. Navy for training and testing purposes. The propulsion system is a solid-fuel ducted rocket ramjet and would not be powerful enough to propel the strike weapon discussed in this study.

6. For information on the level of effort and cost involved with using different types of airframe materials, see Obaid Younossi, Michael Kennedy, and John C. Graser, *Military Airframe Costs: The Effects of Advanced Materials and Manufacturing Processes*, MR-1370-AF, (Arlington, Va.: RAND Project Air Force, 2001).

Table A-3.

Summary of CBO's Cost Estimating Methods for Supersonic Missiles in Alternative 1

	Research and Development	Procurement
Nonrecurring Hardware Design, Testing, and Tooling	Statistical cost estimating relationships were used that relate nonrecurring costs to the average cost of the first 1,000 production units and the time required for development. Also, test results were extrapolated from the JASSM program and increased by 50 percent.	Statistical cost estimating relationships were used that relate nonrecurring costs to the average cost of the first 1,000 production units.
Hardware, Material, and Fabrication		
Engine	Costs were based on information from Hyper-X, SED, and GQM-163 Coyote propulsion hardware.	A step-down factor was estimated on the basis of the cost of this hardware in the research and development phase.
Airframe	A step-up factor was estimated on the basis of the cost of this hardware in the procurement phase.	Costs were based on those for the JSOW system (dollars per pound) and adjusted for weight and materials.
Guidance and control	A step-up factor was estimated on the basis of the cost of this hardware in the procurement phase.	Costs were based on those for the JSOW, SLAM-ER, and Tomahawk systems.
Warhead	A step-up factor was estimated on the basis of the cost of this hardware in the procurement phase.	Costs were based on those for the Tomahawk and other historical missile systems.
Booster rocket	A step-up factor was estimated on the basis of the cost of this hardware in the procurement phase.	The Mk 72 booster was used as an analogy, but costs were adjusted to account for supersonic speeds.
Spares and support equipment	A percentage was added to the cost of all hardware.	A percentage was added to the cost of all hardware.
Other Support	Statistical cost estimating relationships were used that relate support costs to hardware, material, and fabrication costs. Contractor fees were included, which added 15 percent to contractor costs.	Statistical cost estimating relationships were used that relate support costs to hardware, material, and fabrication costs. Contractor fees were included, which added 15 percent to contractor costs.

Source: Congressional Budget Office.

Note: JASSM = Joint Air-to-Surface Standoff Missile; JSOW = Joint Standoff Weapon; SED = Scramjet Engine Demonstration.

CBO relied on data from the production programs of the weapon systems just mentioned to estimate procurement costs for the airframe, the guidance and control system, the warhead, and the rocket booster. CBO adjusted those data to calculate the cost of the first production unit for each of the major components and then applied learning curves to estimate the hardware costs for 2,000 units.[7] For the estimate for the supersonic strike missile, CBO selected a learning curve of 90 percent, consistent with that in five other missile and munitions programs.

In contrast, CBO derived the cost of the engine by estimating the first set of hardware built during the research and development phase (because data on production engines were not available, CBO used engine cost data from development prototypes) and then used a "step-down" equation to estimate the cost of the first production unit. A step-down equation is based on the premise that fabrication in the development phase is usually more expensive because the units are being assembled at lower quantities and do not always have the benefit of special manufacturing tools and other efficiencies available in the production phase. For this estimate, CBO used an equation based on historical missile costs that relates the cost of the first unit in the development phase to the cost of the first unit in the production phase.[8] After estimating

the cost of the first production engine, CBO applied a production learning curve to estimate the cost to procure 2,000 engines.

In addition to the 2,000 production units, CBO assumed 60 missiles would be built in the development phase. The Air Force would use those missiles to test and validate the missile design. Except for their engines, the cost of hardware, material, and fabrication for missiles built in the development phase was estimated using "step-up" equations, which are the inverse of step-down equations. CBO then estimated the cost of the 60 development missiles using a learning curve similar to that used for the production missiles.

To complete the cost estimates for hardware, material, and fabrication, CBO added costs for final integration and system checkout, initial spares, and support equipment (such as containers to transport the missiles). Those estimates were based on factors derived from other missile programs that were applied to the recurring hardware costs.

Nonrecurring Design, Testing, and Tooling

This category includes all of the one-time costs that are not necessarily dependent on the total number of missiles that would be purchased. It includes initial design and engineering efforts, systems testing and evaluation (including flight-testing), tools to build missiles, software development, and efforts to integrate the missile with a delivery aircraft. CBO estimated that the nonrecurring costs for the missile hardware in the research and development phase would total about $800 million.

About 85 percent of the nonrecurring costs in the research and development phase are for initial design and engineering as well as systems testing and evaluation. Design and engineering estimates are based on a statistical relationship that relates the cost of those efforts to the length of the development phase and the average cost of the first 1,000 production units. For that estimate, CBO assumed that the development effort would last about eight years on the basis of the development time of other

---

7. Learning curves are based on the theory that each production unit will be easier to produce than the previous unit because of the increased experience of workers and other efficiencies. The curve is generally expressed as a logarithmic relationship; however, it is frequently described as a percentage decrease in cost or labor hours each time the number of units produced doubles. For this estimate, CBO used a learning curve of 90 percent, which means the hardware for the second unit would cost 90 percent of the cost of the first unit, and the fourth unit would cost 90 percent of the cost of the second unit, and so on. A learning curve equation can also incorporate a coefficient to account for efficiencies gained by increasing the production rate. For this estimate, CBO used a rate coefficient of 95 percent and assumed that the 2,000 missiles would be purchased in lots of approximately 175 each year.

8. For this cost estimate, CBO used step-up/step-down factors and equations contained in Paul L. Hardin and Daniel Nussbaum, *Analysis of the Relationship Between Development and Production Costs and Comparisons with Other Related Step-up/Step-down Studies* (Arlington, Va.: Naval Center for Cost Analysis, January 1994).

missile systems, with additional allowance for the design and testing of new technologies.[9]

CBO used several methods to estimate costs for systems testing and evaluation, including a statistical relationship that uses missile weight and development time as independent variables, as well as actual costs from the Air Force's Joint Air-to-Surface Standoff Missile (JASSM) program. Because the United States does not currently use ramjets in its tactical missiles, data from historical programs may not accurately estimate the cost of testing that new technology. To account for that uncertainty, CBO increased by 50 percent the estimates for systems testing and evaluation produced using the historical data.

Although most nonrecurring costs are incurred in the research and development phase, CBO estimated that there would be about $170 million in nonrecurring costs in the procurement phase for the special tooling and facilities needed for full-rate production of the missile. CBO estimated those costs using a statistical relationship that relates such tooling and facilities costs to missile hardware costs.

Other Support
CBO estimated that other support costs would total $590 million in the research and development phase and $960 million in the procurement phase. Those costs comprise expenses for data collection, contractor fees and program management expenses, warranties and initial

maintenance plans, and government program management expenses.

Program management is the largest component of that category. For the research and development phase, CBO estimated those costs using a statistical cost estimating relationship that incorporates the development time and nonrecurring design costs as independent variables. For the procurement phase, program management is generally a percentage of the recurring hardware costs adjusted for the lot number because program management costs are generally higher in earlier procurement lots.

Contractor fees are another large component of other support costs. For that estimate, CBO assumed that contractor fees would be 15 percent of contractor costs in both the research and development and procurement phases.

The Cost of Bomber Aircraft
CBO also estimated the cost of developing and producing four types of bomber aircraft to provide long-range strike capability: a medium-range subsonic bomber, a medium-range supersonic bomber, a long-range subsonic bomber, and a long-range supersonic bomber (see Table A-4 for a listing of the notional characteristics of those aircraft).

In Alternative 2, the Air Force would develop and purchase a stealthy medium-range subsonic bomber with an empty weight of 60,000 pounds that would be able to carry a payload of 20,000 pounds to a range of 1,500 nautical miles without refueling.[10] It would be able to cruise at speeds of around Mach 0.85 using two engines that would be derived from existing engine designs, such as the General Electric F118 currently used to power the B-2 bomber. By CBO's estimates, the cost to develop such an aircraft would total approximately $19 billion and the cost to purchase 275 of those bombers—enough to replace the current fleet of F-15E and F-117 strike aircraft—would total $52 billion.

---

9. For this estimate, CBO included only those development costs that would be incurred once the initiation of a formal acquisition program had begun. Generally, the estimates include all costs associated with the "system development and demonstration phase" of the updated DoD Directive 5000 (DoD Directive 5000.1, "The Defense Acquisition System," October 23, 2000). However, the estimates include some costs in the "concept and technology demonstration phase," because those activities were included in "program definition and risk reduction activities" prior to the update of DoD 5000 in October 2000. The estimates do not include current and planned expenditures needed to bring the necessary technologies to maturity. For instance, the Air Force, Navy, and Defense Advanced Research Projects Agency will all be contributing hundreds of millions of dollars over the next several years to research various ramjet/scramjet technologies to prove that they have practical applications for a variety of military weapon systems. Those costs are not included here.

10. Empty weight comprises the weight of the airframe, engines, avionics and electronics, weapons, and other support equipment. It excludes the weights of the crew, payload, fuel, and oil.

Table A-4.

Characteristics of Bomber Aircraft

	Alternative 2	Alternative 3	Alternative 4	Alternative 5
Empty Weight (Thousands of pounds)	60	59	128	165
Maximum Speed	Mach 0.85	Mach 1.5	Mach 0.85	Mach 2.4
Payload (Thousands of pounds)	20	10	40	40
Range (Unrefueled, in nautical miles)[a]	1,500	1,500	2,500	2,500
Engine Design	Derivative	Derivative	Derivative	New
Number of Engines	2	2	2	4
Afterburning Engine	No	Yes	No	Yes

Source: Congressional Budget Office.

Note: Alternative 2 = Medium-range subsonic bomber
Alternative 3 = Medium-range supersonic dash bomber
Alternative 4 = Long-range subsonic bomber
Alternative 5 = Long-range supersonic cruise bomber

a.   The ranges shown are the maximum distance from an air base or launcher location to the target. For the aircraft alternatives, the total distance flown on a maximum-range mission would be double the values shown.

In Alternative 3, the Air Force would develop and purchase a stealthy medium-range supersonic bomber conceptually based on either the F-22 or YF-23 fighter.[11] It would have an empty weight of 59,000 pounds and be able to carry a payload of 10,000 pounds to a range of 1,500 nautical miles without refueling. Using two engines based on an existing design such as the F-22's afterburner-equipped Pratt and Whitney F119, it would be able to cruise at subsonic speeds of around Mach 0.85 and dash to speeds in excess of the speed of sound—up to Mach 1.5—although the bomber's range would be reduced substantially when flying at speeds faster than Mach 1.0. According to CBO's estimates, the cost to develop such an aircraft would total approximately $23 billion and the cost to purchase 275 of those bombers would total $61 billion.

In Alternative 4, the Air Force would develop and purchase a highly stealthy long-range subsonic bomber with an empty weight of 128,000 pounds that would be able

to carry a payload of 40,000 pounds to a range of 2,500 nautical miles without refueling. It would be able to cruise at speeds of about Mach 0.85 using improved versions of existing engines, such as the General Electric F118. Those improvements and other changes would allow the use of two engines on this new aircraft, compared with the four used to power the B-2 bomber. By CBO's estimates, the cost to develop such an aircraft would total approximately $31 billion and the cost to purchase 150 of those bombers—enough to replace the current fleet of B-52 and B-1 bomber aircraft—would total $61 billion.

In Alternative 5, the Air Force would develop and purchase a long-range supersonic cruise bomber with an empty weight of 165,000 pounds that would be able to carry a payload of 40,000 pounds to a range of 2,500 nautical miles without refueling. It would be capable of cruising at Mach 2.4 using four newly designed engines. Although this aircraft would employ some stealth features, it would not rely on stealth as extensively as the slower bombers described above. The cost to develop such an aircraft would total approximately $69 billion and the cost to purchase 150 of those bombers would total $137 billion, CBO estimates (see Table A-5 for a summary of the costs to acquire the aircraft described above).

---

11. The F-22 fighter was designed by Lockheed Martin for the Air Force's advanced tactical fighter program and was selected by the Air Force for further development and production. The YF-23 fighter was the design submitted by the team of Northrop Grumman and McDonnell-Douglas.

Table A-5.

Acquisition Costs of Aircraft in Alternatives 2, 3, 4, and 5

	Alternative 2	Alternative 3	Alternative 4	Alternative 5
Research and Development				
Concept and technology development	5	4	3	4
Systems development				
Airframe	5	7	9	25
Engine	1	1	4	4
Avionics	3	4	7	15
Other development	5	7	8	21
Subtotal, development	19	23	31	69
Procurement				
Flyaway				
Airframe	24	27	28	63
Engine	2	4	2	5
Avionics	5	6	6	13
Other procurement costs	21	24	25	56
Subtotal, procurement	52	61	61	137
Military Construction	1	1	1	1
Total Estimated Acquisition Costs	**72**	**85**	**93**	**207**
Memorandum:				
Quantity of Aircraft Procured	275	275	150	150

Source: Congressional Budget Office.

Note: Alternative 2 = Medium-range subsonic bomber
Alternative 3 = Medium-range supersonic dash bomber
Alternative 4 = Long-range subsonic bomber
Alternative 5 = Long-range supersonic cruise bomber

The models and equations CBO used to develop the aircraft characteristics were discussed in Chapter 2. CBO estimated the costs to develop and procure each of the bomber aircraft described above using a common set of estimating methodologies (see Table A-6 for a summary of those methods).

Research and Development Costs

Research and development costs include several components: concept and technology development; engineering design; and other development costs such as prototype manufacturing, testing and evaluation, systems engineering and program management, integrated logistics support, contractor fees, and government program management.

Concept and technology development includes the exploration of early approaches and designs needed to provide certain capabilities, as well as the development of new technologies and components needed to enable the new system to meet performance parameters. CBO estimated those costs using analogies to other aircraft development programs such as the B-2 bomber, F/A-18 fighter, and the F-22 fighter. In developing those estimates, CBO also considered whether the concept development effort would most likely be awarded to multiple contractors, as well as whether flying prototypes would be built. (For instance, contractors Boeing and Lockheed Martin were both hired to develop technology and designs for the Joint Strike Fighter and built flying prototypes as part of the competition to determine which design would be selected for the systems development and demonstration phase.)

Table A-6.

Summary of CBO's Cost Estimating Methods for Aircraft in Alternatives 2, 3, 4, and 5

	Research and Development	Procurement
Hardware, Material, and Fabrication		
Airframe	A statistical cost estimating relationship developed by RAND was used to calculate engineering and design hours on the basis of an aircraft's empty weight and maximum speed, adjusted for the cost of working with advanced materials.	A statistical cost estimating relationship developed by RAND was used to calculate the cumulative average cost of materials, engineering hours, tooling hours, manufacturing hours, and quality assurance hours for 100 aircraft on the basis of an aircraft's empty weight and maximum speed, adjusted for the cost of working with advanced materials.
Engine	A statistical cost estimating relationship developed by RAND was used to calculate the cost of engine development on the basis of engine rotor inlet temperature, specific fuel consumption, the number of test hours, and whether the engine was derived from an existing design.	A statistical cost estimating relationship developed by RAND was used to calculate the theoretical cost to produce the first engine (that cost was based on engine rotor inlet temperature, the aircraft's empty weight, and whether the engine was equipped with an afterburner). Costs for total production were estimated using a 90 percent learning curve.
Avionics	Costs were calculated as a percentage of the cost to develop the engine and airframe, using as a basis the Joint Strike Fighter and F-22 development programs.	Costs were calculated as a percentage of the cost to develop the engine and airframe, using as a basis the B-2, F/A-18E/F, and F-22 development programs.
Spares and support equipment	Not applicable.	Costs were calculated as 15 percent and 30 percent, respectively, of other hardware costs on the basis of average costs for other aircraft acquisition programs.
Other Support		
Testing and evaluation	A statistical cost estimating relationship developed by the Naval Cost Analysis Division was used to calculate flight-test costs on the basis of the aircraft's unit weight, maximim speed, and flight-test hours plus the cost of producing test aircraft, which was stepped up from the production cost estimate.	Not applicable.
Program management	Costs were calculated as a percentage of the sum of airframe costs and testing and evaluation costs.	Costs were calculated as a percentage of airframe costs.
Integrated logistics support	Costs were calculated as a percentage of the sum of airframe costs and testing and evaluation costs.	Not applicable.

Source: Congressional Budget Office.

Engineering design includes the cost to design the airframe, engines, and electronic systems, as well as the cost to design the special tools and manufacturing equipment needed to build each of those components. CBO estimated airframe development costs using a cost estimating relationship formulated by RAND that takes into account the empty weight and maximum speed of the aircraft being designed, as well as the use of advanced materials such as titanium and carbon-thermoset composites in the design.[12] CBO estimated engine development costs using another RAND cost estimating relationship that relates engineering development costs to the engine's rotor inlet temperature, the engine's specific fuel consumption, and the number of engine test hours in the development program. That method also takes into account whether the engine design will be derived from an existing engine or will be a brand new design.[13,14]

Analysts have developed several estimating relationships for calculating the cost to develop avionics systems, but the use of those methods requires extensive design specifications and other technology factors. Those specifications are not usually available for systems in the early concept phase, such as those considered in this study. Instead, CBO used the ratio of the total hardware development costs to the avionics development costs for the F-22 and the Joint Strike Fighter program to estimate avionics development costs for the bomber-aircraft alternatives. Although not as accurate as detailed cost estimating relationships, that method should produce a reasonable estimate of costs.

According to a study by the Institute for Defense Analyses, aircraft that feature a significant number of components that reduce the aircraft's radio frequency and infrared signature cost approximately 30 percent more to design and build than do similarly sized aircraft without such components.[15] Thus, CBO increased the estimated costs for airframe, engine, and avionics development by 30 percent to account for the additional effort required to design the stealth features and the additional cost to develop the techniques and tools needed to manufacture those complex components.

Other development costs include the cost of testing and evaluation, systems engineering and program management (SE/PM), integrated logistics support, contractor fees, and government program management costs. Testing and evaluation costs include the cost of the flight-test program as well as the cost to build prototype airplanes and other equipment needed for testing. CBO estimated flight-test costs using a cost estimating relationship developed by the Navy that relates airframe weight, maximum speed, and the number of flight-test hours to the cost of testing and evaluation. CBO estimated the cost of prototypes using its aircraft production estimating methodology, which is discussed later in this section.

Both SE/PM and integrated-logistics-support estimates are based on a cost estimating relationship developed by the Navy that estimates those costs as a factor of airframe development and testing and evaluation. CBO estimated contractor fees—on the basis of proposals for other aircraft acquisition programs—at 15 percent of the sum of the development costs discussed above. Government program management costs were estimated at 75 percent of systems engineering and contractor program management costs plus 20 percent of systems test and evaluation costs.

Finally, those costs were adjusted to account for cost growth during the time required to develop the aircraft. Research by RAND and the Government Accountability Office has demonstrated that cost analysts systematically underestimate the cost of developing and procuring major weapon systems. That tendency is particularly pronounced in estimates performed in the concept development and early design phases. In a study of 115 major defense acquisition systems, RAND calculated that, on average, estimates of development and procurement costs were too low by 25 percent and 18 percent, respec-

---

12. Younossi, Kennedy, and Graser, *Military Airframe Costs: The Effects of Advanced Materials and Manufacturing Processes.*

13. The rotor inlet temperature is defined as the temperature of the fuel/air combustion products as they enter the first section of rotating engine blades after leaving the stationary blades just aft of the combustion chamber. Higher rotor inlet temperatures are associated with higher thrust-to-weight or power-to-weight ratios. Specific fuel consumption for turbojet or turbofan engines is the ratio of the fuel flow rate to thrust generated—that is, pounds of fuel per hour to pounds of thrust. Lower ratios indicate more-efficient engines.

14. Obaid Younossi and others, *Military Jet Engine Acquisition: Technology Basics and Cost-Estimating Methodology* (Santa Monica, Calif.: RAND Project Air Force, 2002).

15. Bruce R. Harmon and others, *Cost Estimating for Modern Combat Aircraft: Adjusting Existing Databases and Methods to Include Low-Observable Cost Consideration* (Alexandria, Va.: Institute for Defense Analyses, 2001).

tively.[16] To account for that systematic bias, CBO increased the estimate of development costs by 25 percent.

Procurement Costs

Procurement cost estimates include flyaway costs—the recurring costs to manufacture and assemble the airframe, engine, and avionics systems—and other procurement costs, both recurring and nonrecurring. Other recurring costs include program management expenses, contractor fees, and other government costs. Nonrecurring procurement costs include the cost to set up the production facilities, tools, and manufacturing equipment. They also include the cost of support equipment that is unique to the airplane; simulators for pilot training; maintenance manuals and technical publications; and an initial complement of spare parts.

CBO estimated airframe costs using cost estimating relationships developed by RAND that predict costs on the basis of inputs such as the aircraft's empty weight, its speed, and the increased cost of working with advanced materials such as titanium and carbon thermosets. Engine costs were estimated using another RAND cost estimating relationship that considers factors such as the engine's weight and its rotor inlet temperature. That equation also accounts for the cost of producing engines equipped with an afterburner.[17] CBO calculated avionics costs as a percentage of total hardware costs on the basis of the ratio of those costs from the F-22 and F/A-18 programs.[18] On the basis of the study by the Institute for Defense Analyses, CBO increased its estimate of the costs of the airframe, engine, and avionics by 30 percent to account for the additional effort of working with special stealth materials and structures designed to reduce the aircraft's radar, thermal, visual, and electromagnetic signature.

---

16. J.A. Drezner and others, *An Analysis of Weapon System Cost Growth* (Santa Monica, Calif.: RAND Project Air Force, 1993).

17. Younossi and others, *Military Jet Engine Acquisition: Technology Basics and Cost-Estimating Methodology.*

18. Estimates of costs for avionics and electronics are often developed through the use of complex proprietary cost models like PRICE or through cost estimating relationships with inputs such as avionics weight or the level of technology integration. CBO did not define the avionics systems in the detail needed to use those cost estimating relationships. Rather, CBO estimated avionics costs as a percentage of total airframe and engine costs on the basis of recent production programs for high-performance aircraft such as the F-22 and the F/A-18 E/F.

CBO used two factors to estimate other recurring procurement costs. Combined program management costs for the contractor and the government are approximately 11 percent of airframe procurement costs, whereas the contractor's fee is estimated as 15 percent of other production costs for the contractor.

CBO used two methods to estimate other nonrecurring procurement costs. On the basis of actual costs from other aircraft acquisition programs, CBO estimated costs for other support equipment and initial spare parts at 30 percent and 15 percent of flyaway costs, respectively. CBO used a cost estimating relationship developed by the Navy to estimate the cost of special tools and test equipment at roughly 1.5 percent of the costs of airframe procurement.

On the basis of the RAND study on cost growth in weapon-system acquisitions, CBO increased all procurement costs by 15 percent to account for that factor.

Military Construction

Because the bombers in CBO's alternatives would replace existing planes, CBO assumed that many of the facilities used to house and maintain those aircraft would be available to support the new aircraft. However, the introduction of any new weapon system will require some new facilities or significant modifications to existing facilities. For instance, new buildings for simulators are often needed, and existing hangars may require modifications if they are not of the proper dimensions to accommodate new aircraft. On the basis of actual military construction costs for other aircraft acquisition programs, CBO estimated that such costs could range from $500 million to $1 billion, depending on the similarity between the new system and the aircraft it would replace. For that estimate, CBO included $1 billion in construction costs for each alternative.

Results

The costs to develop and acquire the four aircraft platforms considered for providing long-range strike capability would range from $72 billion to $207 billion.

Alternative 2. Acquiring 275 medium-range subsonic bombers would cost $72 billion, CBO estimates. In CBO's estimate, developing the aircraft accounts for $19 billion, or 26 percent of the total acquisition costs. Concept development accounts for $5 billion of those costs, including the cost to build several flying prototypes, whereas the cost to develop the airframe, a derivative engine, and avionics account for another $9 billion. Other development costs account for the remaining $5 billion.

Procurement costs, estimated at $52 billion, would be 72 percent of the acquisition costs. By CBO's estimates, it would cost $31 billion to produce 275 aircraft. Other production costs would total $21 billion. Military construction costs would account for the remaining 2 percent of acquisition costs. On average, each aircraft would cost $261 million to acquire.

Alternative 3. Acquiring 275 medium-range supersonic dash bombers would cost $85 billion, CBO estimates. Developing the aircraft would cost $23 billion, or 27 percent of the total acquisition costs. Including the cost to build several flying prototypes, concept development would account for $4 billion of those costs, slightly less than those for Alternative 2 because CBO assumed that some of the necessary development work had already been accomplished under the F-22 and the YF-23 programs. The cost to develop the airframe, a derivative engine, and avionics would account for another $12 billion. Other development costs would account for the remaining $7 billion.

Procurement costs of $61 billion would account for 72 percent of the acquisition costs, including $37 billion to build the aircraft, CBO estimates. Other procurement costs would total $24 billion. Military construction costs would account for the remaining 1 percent of acquisition costs. On average, each aircraft would cost $307 million to acquire.

Alternative 4. By CBO's estimates, it would cost $93 billion to acquire 150 long-range subsonic bombers. Developing the aircraft would cost $31 billion, or 34 percent of the total acquisition costs. In CBO's estimate, concept development would account for $3 billion of those costs, which CBO assumed would not include flying prototypes because of the high cost of building larger airplanes. The cost to develop the airframe, a derivative engine, and avionics account for $20 billion, whereas other development costs account for the remaining $8 billion.

Procurement costs of $61 billion would constitute 65 percent of the acquisition costs. It would cost $36 billion to produce 150 aircraft, CBO estimates. Other procurement costs would total $25 billion. Military construction costs would account for the remaining 1 percent of acqui-

sition costs. On average, the aircraft would cost $627 million to acquire.

Alternative 5. Acquiring 150 long-range supersonic bombers would cost $207 billion, CBO estimates. Developing aircraft would cost $69 billion, or 33 percent of the total acquisition costs. Concept development would represent for $4 billion of those costs, which CBO assumed would not include flying prototypes. The cost to develop the airframe, a new engine, and avionics would account for $44 billion, whereas other development costs would account for the remaining $21 billion.

Procurement costs of $137 billion would make up 66 percent of the acquisition costs. It would cost $81 billion to produce 150 aircraft, CBO estimates. Other procurement costs would total $56 billion. Military construction costs would account for less than 1 percent of acquisition costs. On average, the aircraft would cost $1.38 billion to acquire.

Costs of the Common Aero Vehicle System

The common aero vehicle (CAV) is a maneuverable reentry vehicle that delivers a weapon from space. CBO assumed that the CAV would carry a 1,000-pound warhead designed to penetrate hardened targets. CBO estimated the costs of three alternatives for employing CAVs in the long-range strike mission—two that would deploy CAVs aboard ground-based ballistic missiles and one that would deploy them aboard orbiting satellites.

In Alternative 6, the Army would deploy the CAVs aboard ground-based solid-fuel boosters powered by rocket motors similar to the Orion 50 built by Alliant Techsystems. CBO assumed that the Army would purchase a total of 48 CAVs, 48 rocket boosters, and 24 mobile launchers. Each booster would carry a single CAV, and two boosters would be deployed on each launcher. Four mobile launchers, eight boosters, and eight CAVs would be procured as spares.

In Alternative 7, the Air Force would deploy the CAVs aboard ground-based Peacekeeper missiles that are being retired from use as strategic nuclear ballistic missiles. CBO assumed that the Air Force would purchase a total of 48 CAVs and convert 24 Peacekeepers to launch them. Each missile would carry two CAVs. CBO assumed that

Table A-7.

Characteristics of Common Aero Vehicles in Alternatives 6, 7, and 8

	Alternative 6	Alternative 7	Alternative 8
Launch Platform	Solid rocket booster	Peacekeeper missile	EELV Heavy
Number of CAVs per Platform	1	2	8
Total Number of CAVs Deployed	40	40	40
Number of Spare CAVs	8	8	8
Number of Replacement CAVs	0	0	80
Payload per CAV	1,000-pound warhead	1,000-pound warhead	1,000-pound warhead

Source: Congressional Budget Office.

Note: EELV = Evolved Expendable Launch Vehicle

Alternative 6 = Medium-range surface-based common aero vehicle
Alternative 7 = Long-range surface-based CAV
Alternative 8 = Space-based CAV

10 Peacekeeper missiles would be based at Cape Canaveral Air Station in Florida and 10 missiles would be based at Vandenberg Air Force Base in California. Four missiles and eight CAVs would be used as spares.

In Alternative 8, the Air Force would deploy the CAVs in space aboard satellites that would be placed into orbit by heavy launch vehicles such as the Evolved Expendable Launch Vehicle (EELV). The orbiting CAVs would use a rocket motor to bring them out of orbit to attack targets on Earth. CBO assumed that the Air Force would purchase 128 CAVs and 16 satellites. A constellation of five satellites, each carrying eight CAVs, would be continuously maintained in orbit. Because orbits decay and the harsh environment of space eventually degrades orbiting equipment, CBO assumed that the constellation would be replaced twice during a 30-year period, requiring a total of 120 CAVs and 15 satellites. Eight additional CAVs and one additional satellite would be purchased to replace any that might be lost in a launch failure (see Table A-7 for a description of the technical characteristics of those alternatives).

By CBO's estimates, acquisition costs would total about $4 billion for the ground-based alternatives and about $12 billion for the space alternative (see Table A-8 for a summary of the costs of those alternatives). CBO used several methods, discussed below, to estimate the costs of development, procurement, and facilities construction for those alternative methods of deploying the common

aero vehicles (see Table A-9 for a summary of those methods).

Research and Development Costs

CBO estimated that the cost to develop the CAV weapon system and its various supporting components would total about $2.5 billion for the ground-based alternatives and about $4 billion for the space-based alternative. Those estimates include the costs to develop technology and produce designs for the various system components such as the common aero vehicle, booster vehicles, mobile launchers, rocket motors, orbital support system (protective satellite), and launch vehicles. They also include the cost to test and evaluate those components, as well as the cost to integrate them into a functioning system. There is significant uncertainty about the maturity of the technologies associated with the common aero vehicle, which results in a substantial risk that costs could exceed initial estimates. In its estimates, CBO used research by RAND for comparable systems to account for that risk.

Common Aero Vehicle. CBO used DoD's estimate of the development costs for a program called FALCON (Force Application and Launch from the Continental United States) as the basis for estimating development costs for the CAV. In the program, the Defense Advanced Research Projects Agency and the Air Force are developing hypersonic technologies needed for weapons that can

Table A-8.

Acquisition Costs of Common Aero Vehicles in Alternatives 6, 7, and 8

(Billions of 2006 dollars)

	Alternative 6	Alternative 7	Alternative 8
Research and Development			
Common aero vehicles	0.6	0.6	0.6
Booster vehicles	0.1	0.5	n.a.
Mobile launcher	0.3	n.a.	n.a.
Rocket motors	n.a.	n.a.	0.4
Protective satellites	n.a.	n.a.	0.6
Launch vehicles	n.a.	n.a.	0
Test and evaluation	1.0	1.0	1.7
System integration	0.4	0.4	0.7
Subtotal, research and development	2.4	2.5	4.0
Procurement			
Common aero vehicles	0.5	0.5	1.4
Booster vehicles	0.4	0.3	n.a.
Mobile launcher	0.3	n.a.	n.a.
Rocket motors	n.a.	n.a.	0.1
Protective satellites	n.a.	n.a.	0.7
Launch vehicles	n.a.	n.a.	5.4
Subtotal, procurement	1.2	0.9	7.7
Military Construction	0	0.6	0
Total Estimated Acquisition Costs	**3.7**	**4.0**	**11.7**

Source: Congressional Budget Office.

Note: n.a. = not applicable.

rapidly strike targets over global ranges from launch platforms in the United States. Such technologies would give the United States the capability to build a weapon that could be used to promptly strike distant targets by traveling through space in a suborbital trajectory aboard a hypersonic vehicle. CBO assumed that development efforts for the CAV would be similar, given the common purpose and performance characteristics of those two systems.

Over the next several years, DoD plans continued investment in the program to evaluate the performance of hypersonic technologies in realistic operating environments. The department hopes to launch three test vehicles as part of that program over the 2007-2010 period. On the basis of funding plans for those programs, CBO estimates that it could cost $620 million to develop an operational CAV weapon. That estimate is higher than the one in DoD's plans for two reasons. First, systems en-

gineering and program management efforts of formal acquisition programs typically cost about 33 percent more than such efforts in technology development programs like FALCON. Second, RAND's research on cost growth in defense programs indicates that cost estimates performed early in the development phase tend to understate total development costs for space and missile programs by as much as 40 percent.

Booster Vehicle. In Alternative 6, the Army would use solid-fuel rocket boosters to launch ground-based CAVs into a suborbital trajectory toward the target. On the basis of information from the Army, CBO estimated that it would cost about $140 million to modify existing booster designs to accommodate the CAVs.

In Alternative 7, the Air Force would use Peacekeeper missiles to boost ground-based CAVs onto a suborbital trajectory. Development estimates include the costs to provide a new guidance and navigation system, the costs to modify the missile's propulsion system, and the costs to design a lighter deployment module and shroud.[19] Materials to justify the budget indicate that the Air Force spent about $400 million to design and test similar upgrades to the Minuteman III missile. CBO assumed that the costs of the Peacekeeper modification effort would be somewhat more expensive—about $490 million—to account for cost growth.

Mobile Launcher. Under Alternative 6, two medium-range CAV missiles would be placed aboard one mobile launcher. Mobile-launch vehicles are produced today, although CBO assumed that the CAVs and the solid-fuel rocket booster would need a newly designed canister to provide a stable environment for the missiles and to contain them on the vehicle. On the basis of estimates that were developed in CBO's earlier study on missile defense, CBO estimated that it would cost about $280 million to develop those canisters.[20]

Rocket Motor. CBO used a cost estimating relationship developed by Tecolote to estimate development costs for the rocket motors needed for the space-based alternative.[21] That method uses several factors, including the duration of the development phase, the number of prototypes built during that phase, and the total procurement cost of the rocket motors. CBO estimated that the procurement cost of the rocket motors would total about $140 million. (Derivation of that procurement estimate is discussed in the subsequent section on procurement.) Assuming that the development program for the CAV rocket motor would require 16 prototypes and that the development phase would last 60 months, CBO estimated that developing the rocket motor would cost about $400 million.

Protective Satellite. The protective satellite is the orbital support component of the space-based system that includes a propulsion system to control the satellite's position in orbit and shielding to protect the CAVs from the harsh environment in space. CBO used a cost estimating relationship derived by Technomics that gauges development costs for the protective satellite on the basis of its weight.[22] Assuming that the protective satellite would weigh about 10,900 pounds, CBO estimated that the development of the protective satellite would cost about $610 million.

Launch Vehicles. CBO assumed that the space-based CAVs would be put in orbit aboard rockets that are currently used to launch other military payloads; therefore, no additional development costs for those vehicles were included in this estimate.

Testing and Evaluation. For both ground-based alternatives, CBO assumed that DoD would conduct 16 integrated flight tests of the CAV and the launch vehicle over a four-year period. On the basis of cost estimates for production of CAVs and launch vehicles, CBO estimated that the hardware for those tests would cost almost $200 million. Additionally, information provided by a contractor indicates that support equipment at the test sight, target sets, and test data processing would cost about $400 million. After accounting for cost growth of about 40 percent, CBO estimated that testing and evaluation for either ground-based alternative would cost about $1 billion.

In the flight-test program for the space-based alternative, the Air Force would launch two heavy launch vehicles, each carrying one satellite and eight CAVs. By CBO's estimates, the flight-test program would cost about $1.7 billion—almost double the costs for the ground-based alternatives because of the additional expense of two heavy launch vehicles.

System Integration. For all of the alternatives, CBO assumed that system integration would add 20 percent to the total costs for common aero vehicles, booster vehicles, and mobile launchers—consistent with the costs for existing boosters such as the Minuteman and Peacekeeper programs and the estimated costs for the kinetic energy interceptor program. System integration would cost about $400 million for the ground-based alternatives and about $670 million for the space-based alternative, CBO estimates.

19. The deployment module provides structural support and carries the electronics needed to activate and deploy the CAV, and the shroud protects the CAV during flight.

20. Congressional Budget Office, *Alternatives for Boost-Phase Missile Defense* (July 2004).

21. Tecolote Research, Inc., *The Unmanned Space Vehicle Cost Model*, 8th ed. (Goleta, Calif.: Tecolote Research, June 2002).

22. Technomics, Inc., *National Missile Defense Propulsion Cost Estimating Relationships* (Santa Barbara, Calif.: Technomics, August 2000.)

Table A-9.

Summary of CBO's Cost Estimating Methods for Common Aero Vehicles in Alternatives 6, 7, and 8

	Research and Development	Procurement
Ground-Based Alternatives		
Hardware, Material, and Fabrication		
Common aero vehicles	Costs were estimated using the Air Force's FALCON program with adjustments for additional management and cost risk.	Costs were estimated using the Air Force's Mk 21 reentry vehicle with adjustments for more insulation, heavier mass, and the vehicle's payload and navigation equipment.
Booster vehicles		
Medium-range booster	An Army cost estimate was used to project costs.	A statistical cost estimating relationship was used that relates production costs to a booster's impulse.
Peacekeeper	Costs were based on those for the Minuteman III missile system.	Costs were based on those for the Minuteman III missile system.
Mobile launchers	An Army cost estimate was used to project costs.	Costs were based on a contractor's estimate of the costs for a mobile launcher proposed for use with boost-phase interceptors.
Testing and Evaluation	Costs were based on those for hardware and data processing for 16 tests.	Not applicable.
Systems Integration	A percentage (20 percent) was added to the costs of hardware design and testing and evaluation activities.	Not applicable.

Continued

Procurement Costs

Procurement costs would total between $870 million and $1.2 billion for the ground-based alternatives and about $7.7 billion for the space-based alternative. CBO calculated total procurement costs using a two-step approach—first estimating the costs of producing the first unit of each of the major components and then projecting those costs for the remaining purchases. CBO assumed that the unit price of subsequent CAVs would not decline appreciably because the procurement quantities would be small. In CBO's estimate, procurement costs include the cost of producing the CAVs themselves, as well as the cost of booster vehicles and mobile launchers for the ground-based alternatives and the costs of rocket motors, protective satellites, and launch vehicles for the space-based alternative.

Common Aero Vehicle. CBO used actual procurement costs for the Air Force's Mk 21 reentry vehicle (developed for the Peacekeeper missile) to estimate the procurement costs for the CAV in all three alternatives. However, the CAV would require more thermal protection than would the Mk 21. According to the Air Force, the average cost of the Mk 21 reentry vehicle is about $1 million (assuming a purchase of about 50 of them), divided evenly between the cost for the vehicle's outer shell and the fusing and firing assemblies. CBO increased that cost to account for several technical differences between the notional CAV and the Mk 21 reentry vehicle.

First, CBO increased costs to account for two differences in the physical characteristics—the size of the CAV and the need for greater thermal protection. The Mk 21's reentry vehicle has a conical shape that measures about two feet wide at its base by about six feet tall. CBO assumed

Table A-9.

Continued

	Research and Development	Procurement
	Space-Based Alternatives	
Hardware, Material, and Fabrication		
Common aero vehicles	Costs were estimated using the Air Force's FALCON program with adjustments for additional management and cost risk.	Costs were estimated using the Air Force's Mk 21 reentry vehicle with adjustments for more insulation, heavier mass, and the vehicle's payload and navigation equipment.
Rocket motors	A statistical cost estimating relationship was used that relates design costs to several factors, including procurement costs.	A statistical cost estimating relationship was used that relates production costs to a rocket motor's impulse.
Protective satellites	A statistical cost estimating relationship was used that relates design costs to a satellite's weight.	A statistical cost estimating relationship was used that relates production costs to a satellite's weight.
Launch vehicles	This cost was assumed to be a sunk investment.	Costs were based on those for the Air Force's EELV heavy launch vehicle.
Testing and Evaluation	Costs were based on those for hardware and data processing for 16 tests.	Not applicable.
Systems Integration	A percentage (20 percent) was added to the costs of hardware design and test and evaluation activities.	Not applicable.

Source: Congressional Budget Office.

Note: FALCON = Force Application and Launch from the Continental United States; EELV = Evolved Expendable Launch Vehicle.

that the CAV would measure three feet by 15 feet and would have three to four times more surface area than would the Mk 21 reentry vehicle. CBO estimated that the difference would increase costs by a factor of 3.4, assuming that costs were proportional to surface area.

Whereas the Mk 21 follows a ballistic trajectory toward the target, the CAV would glide and maneuver toward the target after it reentered the atmosphere, subjecting it to greater mechanical stresses and higher temperatures for a longer period of time. On the basis of information provided by a contractor, CBO estimated that the CAV would require about two inches of insulation beneath the surface coating used on the Mk 21 reentry vehicles. On the basis of discussions with industry analysts, CBO estimated that the price of the insulation would be about one-third the cost of the coating. After accounting for those physical characteristics and the cost for the surface

coating and insulating materials, CBO calculated that the cost of the thermal protection for the CAV would be about 2.6 times more per square foot than the cost of thermal protection for the Mk 21 reentry vehicles. After increasing the average cost of the Mk 21 shell by both the surface area and thickness factors and increasing the average cost of the fusing and firing assemblies by the surface area factor only, CBO estimated that those components would cost between $4 million and $5 million per CAV.

Second, CBO increased the costs of the CAV to account for an onboard navigation and guidance system. Such systems are components of the Minuteman missile itself; thus, their costs are not included in the price of the Mk 21 reentry vehicle. CBO's estimate of those costs was based on the actual procurement costs of current-generation guidance and navigation equipment for the Minuteman III missiles. According to budget materials, the most recent purchase of guidance and navigation equipment for the Minuteman missile cost between $2 million and $3 million.

Third, CBO included in the estimate the costs for a 1,000-pound warhead that would be deployed on the CAV. CBO's estimate of about $6,000 per warhead is based on the average cost for such devices according to the Air Force's budget materials.

Finally, CBO increased costs to account for historical cost growth for comparable systems. On the basis of a report by RAND, CBO estimated that production costs for the CAV could grow by 38 percent.[23] Thus, CBO estimated that the average cost of the CAV would total about $11 million. For the two ground-based alternatives, CBO estimated that it would cost about $540 million to buy 48 CAVs. That estimate includes the cost to integrate the CAV with the other components of the weapon system— about 12 percent of hardware costs based on experience with other comparable programs. For the space-based alternative, CBO assumed that DoD would buy a total of 128 CAVs at a cost of $1.4 billion.

Booster Vehicle. In Alternative 6, CBO assumed that each solid rocket booster would carry a single CAV and that two boosters would be loaded on each mobile launcher. On the basis of a cost estimating relationship that relates booster thrust to cost, CBO estimated that each booster would cost about $9 million, including about $1 million for the canister to contain the booster on the mobile launcher. That estimate also includes a factor of about 38 percent for cost growth. In total, CBO estimated that buying 48 boosters would cost about $420 million.

In Alternative 7, the Air Force would deploy the CAVs aboard Peacekeeper missiles. CBO estimated that each Peacekeeper missile would be able to carry two CAVs; therefore, a total of 24 missiles would need to be modified—20 for operations and four for spares. (On the basis of information from the Air Force, CBO estimated that there are about 60 Peacekeeper missiles in the U.S. inventory.) CBO assumed that the modifications would include upgrading the missile's propulsion and guidance

system, buying a new deployment module, and buying a new shroud. As a point of comparison, actual costs for upgrading the propulsion and guidance system for the Minuteman III missile averaged about $6 million per missile. Assuming that the costs for upgrading the Peacekeeper missiles' propulsion and guidance system would be comparable with those costs, and adding $4 million for the costs to procure a new deployment module and a new shroud, CBO estimated that the costs to modify each Peacekeeper missile would total about $14 million. That estimate includes a cost-growth factor of 38 percent. In total, CBO estimated that modifying 24 Peacekeeper missiles would cost about $330 million.

Mobile Launcher. In Alternative 6, the CAVs would be placed aboard a mobile launcher that would carry two medium-range CAV missiles. For this analysis, CBO used a cost estimate that was developed in an earlier study on boost-phase interceptors.[24] In that study, CBO estimated that a mobile launcher capable of firing two interceptors would cost a little more than $11 million in 2004 dollars. After adjusting for inflation, CBO estimated that each mobile launcher would cost slightly less than $12 million in 2006 dollars, or about $280 million for 24 mobile launchers.

Rocket Motor. In Alternative 8, the space-based CAVs would use a rocket motor to reenter the Earth's atmosphere. CBO applied a cost estimating relationship developed by Technomics that relates a rocket motor's procurement costs to the product of its total impulse expressed in newtons of thrust and its burn time expressed in seconds. CBO estimated that a rocket motor with a thrust of 113 kilo newtons and a burn time of five seconds would cost just over $1 million to produce.[25] That estimate also includes a factor of 19 percent to account for growth observed in the cost estimates of comparable space-based systems.

CBO assumed that the rocket motors would be bought over the same time period as would the CAVs and that the cost per rocket motor would remain essentially unchanged over the production period. Buying 128 rocket

23. Jeanne M. Jarvaise, Jeffrey A. Drezner, and Daniel M. Norton, *The Defense System Cost Performance Database: Cost Growth Analysis Using Selected Acquisition Reports,* MR-625-OSD (Santa Monica, Calif.: RAND, 1996).

24. Congressional Budget Office, *Alternatives for Boost-Phase Missile Defense.*

25. Technomics, Inc., *National Missile Defense Propulsion Cost Estimating Relationships.*

motors (one for each of the CAVs) would cost a total of about $140 million, CBO estimates.

Protective Satellite. CBO applied a cost estimating relationship developed by Tecolote that uses the weight of the protective satellite to estimate the cost to procure the protective satellite. CBO assumed that the protective satellite would weigh about half as much as the combined weight of the eight CAVs. Eight CAVs and their rocket motors would weigh about 21,800 pounds; therefore, the protective satellite would weigh about 10,900 pounds. CBO estimated that each protective satellite would cost about $45 million.

CBO assumed that the protective satellites would be bought over the same time period as would the CAVs and rocket motors. Buying the 16 protective satellites (one for every eight CAVs) would cost about $720 million, CBO estimates.

Launch Vehicle. The space-based CAV system would be put in orbit by a launch vehicle. CBO estimated that each satellite—consisting of one protective satellite and eight CAVs—would weigh about 16 tons. CBO assumed that the CAV system would be launched aboard a heavy launch vehicle currently planned for the Air Force's EELV

program and assumed that DoD would place one CAV satellite aboard each launch vehicle. CBO estimated the procurement costs for the launch vehicle on the basis of budget data provided by the Air Force. Those data indicate that the costs for a launch vehicle would total about $340 million, including about $190 million for the vehicle hardware and about $150 million for the launch services. CBO estimated that the costs for 16 launch vehicles—one CAV satellite on each heavy launch vehicle—would total about $5.4 billion.

Military Construction Costs

Under Alternative 7, CBO assumed that the Air Force would make improvements to facilities at Cape Canaveral Air Station and Vandenberg Air Force Base, the bases where the Peacekeeper/CAV systems would be deployed. At each base, the Air Force would install new equipment to support ground operations and build 10 new silos to house the Peacekeeper missiles. Support equipment would cost about $50 million per set, and the missile silos would cost about $15 million each. After applying a factor of 50 percent to account for cost growth, CBO estimated that it would cost $600 million for silos and support equipment at the two bases.

www.ingramcontent.com/pod-product-compliance
Lightning Source LLC
Chambersburg PA
CBHW080851010626

R18375900001B/R183759PG45790CBX00005B/9